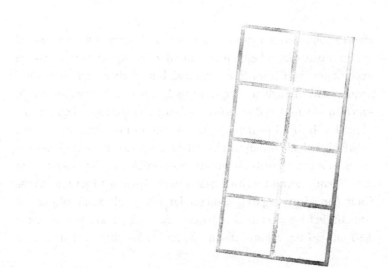

Through a Dog's Eyes

Through a Dog's Eyes

Jennifer Arnold

Souvenir Press

In loving memory of Nicholas, my forever dog.

*The greatness of a nation and its moral progress
can be judged by the way its animals are treated.*

—Mahatma Gandhi

CONTENTS

As the founder and executive director of Canine Assistants, a non-profit service-dog school based just north of Atlanta, I have spent the past twenty years working with dogs and I have become convinced they are the most giving of all creatures. There is no question that dogs give their trust, strength, affection, and adoration to the people they love. I have witnessed many dog-made miracles in my work, and with each day I find more to love about these amazing animals.

Over time, I have learned a tremendous amount about how dogs perceive the world. I have also come to hold very strong convictions about how they should be treated—always with kindness and respect. I am deeply concerned and disappointed with the dog-management methods that have recently gained popularity. Training methodologies, once headed in the direction of kindness and respect, have largely reversed course over the past several years. It is common now to hear people speak of the supposed need to dominate and become physically controlling "alpha types" when handling dogs. Also making a comeback, sadly, are certain types of collars that cause dogs pain and discomfort, such as shock collars and choke chains. What happened here? I may never fully understand what caused the shift, but there is one thing I do understand: This cruelty must be stopped.

This book replicates, to a large extent, my journey of discovery about dogs. So many of the things that I did wrong with my dogs early in my career happened because I simply did not know better. I saw forceful methods being used with dogs all around me. I was told that in order to be "good with dogs" you had to be tough with them. Now I know how wrong this is *and* why it is so wrong. I want all dog owners to know what I have learned. Knowledge and understanding will lead you to a far kinder way of handling your dog and a much happier life for both of you.

Throughout this book, I will be making assertions about dogs with which a few scientists may disagree. For example, some scientists do not yet feel there is conclusive evidence that dogs have thoughts or emotions. While it may be difficult to prove such a thing scientifically, to those who live with dogs, these assertions are a given. This book is directed toward those of us who love dogs and is not intended to be fuel for scientific debate, so I am going to subscribe to a theory best summed up by an old Southernism: "If it waddles like a duck and quacks like a duck, it probably ain't a pigeon."

Those who endorse differing methodologies and whose economic interests will be threatened by my approach may well direct their wrath my way, but that will not deter me. Dogs manage to maintain an unwavering trust that human beings are good despite our occasional behavior to the contrary. It is long past time for us to honor their trust.

As I write this, my four big dogs surround me. Jack, my four-year-old goldendoodle, lies closest to me, his big head resting on my right foot. Nan and Margaret Ann, both twelve-year-old golden retrievers, lie back to back in the sunny spot just to my left. Butch, a mix like Jack and the baby at eighteen months, is behind me, rolled onto his back, so completely relaxed he looks almost boneless. I like to think that my presence allows them to rest so peacefully. I know that their presence and their unconditional trust inspire me to continue writing even when a beautiful spring day tempts me outside.

Through a Dog's Eyes

CHAPTER ONE

Beginnings

Early one cool September morning when I was sixteen years old, I jumped out of my bed, headed for the bathroom. A split second after my feet hit the floor, my bottom followed. I knew I hadn't tripped or fallen over anything. When I tried to stand, I found that my legs would not hold me up. I remember feeling totally confused. What I didn't realize at the time and couldn't possibly know was that I'd just taken the first step of a lifelong journey that would ultimately provide me with a remarkable gift.

The diagnosis was multiple sclerosis, and the prognosis was that I would likely never walk again. I fell apart. As a teenager, the most important thing to me was being with my friends, something that suddenly seemed impossible. I was particularly upset because the school I had attended my whole life wasn't wheelchair accessible, which meant that I wouldn't be graduating the following year with my class. I was convinced that any kind of life worth living was over. In retrospect, having met incredible people through my work whose wheelchairs have never slowed them down, I am ashamed of the way I reacted. I am grateful that my work has given me the opportunity to learn that being "healed" and feeling "well" isn't so much a physical process as an emotional one.

I was the youngest of four children. As my dad's medical practice was well established by the time I came along, I had the privilege of spending a great deal more time with him than had my brother and sisters. Dad and I would take long walks, play tennis, and go fishing at a nearby lake. I adored my mom, but Dad and I were best buddies. Neither of us was prepared for the shock that September morning brought. My sudden illness was particularly hard on him. More than the physical implications, he worried about my mental health, I think. Dad realized that I needed to have something on which to focus, something hopeful.

As fate would have it, he had recently read about a woman in California who was training dogs to help people who used wheelchairs. Knowing how much I loved animals and hoping to give me a reason to keep fighting, he contacted the woman. Unfortunately, she couldn't send a dog as far as my hometown of Atlanta. Rather than being disappointed, Dad grew determined. He decided that a similar program was surely needed in our part of the country. On the Friday after Thanksgiving, he met with a CPA about setting up a nonprofit program he named Canine Assistants. Three weeks later, Dad was walking on the sidewalk along a nearby park when a drunk driver on a motorcycle jumped onto the path and hit him.

All night, I stayed in the waiting room of the ICU of the hospital where Dad was on staff. His coworkers flooded the hospital. He was not only a gifted surgeon, he was a wonderful man, and his friends were using all their skills to keep him alive. We kept hoping for good news that night, though it never came. Dad was broken. The hands he had used to give sight to so many were literally crushed. His brilliant brain was damaged. For most of the night, his blood pressure was almost nonexistent. Toward morning, nature overrode the heroics of modern medicine, and my dad died.

The only thing that kept me from falling into despair was my anger. If you've ever faced such dark anguish, you know what a blessing anger can be. I had to fight the adversity or die myself. I decided the best reason to continue living was to make the world better for someone else who was hurting; otherwise, life seemed like a pointless exercise in pain. I grabbed the dream of Canine Assistants and I held it like a lifeline.

Over the next several years, my illness went into full remission and I slowly regained the ability to walk. How? I was lucky. That is the best answer I have. My doctors conjectured about why my condition improved so much, but then and now that seems unimportant to me. The simple fact is clear: I got lucky.

Mom and I were not so lucky when it came to money. There was a clause in Dad's life-insurance policy that negated payout in cases of "death by two-wheeled vehicle," which was obviously intended for those riding on or driving motorcycles. The insurance company nevertheless enforced the clause in his case. Without the insurance money and the substantial cash flow Dad's medical practice had brought, money became a problem for the first time in our lives. Mom and I learned a great deal about the value of buying in bulk, shopping at discount stores, Sunday morning newspaper coupons, and weekly sales at the local grocery stores. My siblings were just beginning their adult lives, married with young children or otherwise trying to establish themselves, so they were not able to help much financially. We did get help, though, from a number of wonderful people and one remarkable woman in particular.

When I was six months old, my mom found herself thoroughly overwhelmed with four young children and her need to "support" Dad in his medical practice, which meant going out a lot and being pleasant to strangers. Who would have thought that doctors would have to play such games? Anyway, money was starting to come in from Dad's practice, so he suggested that Mom hire someone to help around the house. Through good fortune she hired a woman named Sallie Kate Brooks, one of the finest human beings I have ever known. From the beginning, Nanny, as my brother nicknamed her, was Mom's best friend and another mother to my siblings and me. After Dad died, Nanny continued to come to our home five days a week, even though we could no longer afford to pay her. Often, she would bring bags of vegetables from her husband's garden, and more than a few times she quietly paid the rent we could not afford to pay on the small apartment we now called home. Nanny helped to keep us fed and housed, but she also helped to keep us sane.

Still, it was Mom who was our foundation, the strength that kept us going. Widowed at age forty-eight, with no money, no job experience, and a hurting child, she could have gotten into her bed and pulled the covers over her head, but she didn't. Instead, she found herself a job as the receptionist for an orthopedic surgeon. Mom wasn't very good with the office typing or with the complicated phone system they used, but she was wonderful with the patients. She was one of those rare people who could make you feel like a million dollars just by spending a few minutes with you. And, if she loved you, she loved you completely. She believed so strongly in me and in the dream of Canine Assistants that she never let me quit trying to make the program a reality, pushing me when I didn't think I could go on. A few months ago, someone told me that I reminded her so much of my mother. I cried when I heard those words. I cannot imagine a greater compliment.

As Mom worked in the doctor's office, I took a variety of jobs to contribute to household needs and raise money to start Canine Assistants. I delivered pizzas. I worked in veterinary clinics, which I loved because it allowed me to learn more about dogs. I even went to farrier school and began to shoe horses. There was excellent money to be made shoeing, but my body, still weak from illness, wasn't capable of handling the physical demands of the job. We were getting by but not getting ahead, and my dream of Canine Assistants still seemed far away.

Then something wonderful happened. One day in the spring of 1990, I found a piece of property for sale by its owner about thirty miles north of Atlanta. It had several small houses, a barn, fields for the dogs to run in, and, best of all, appropriate zoning. It was the perfect place to start Canine Assistants. Just one minor problem—money. Mom and I had no credit history, so we had no ability to borrow from a bank. All I could think to do was ask the man who owned the property to finance it for us—something he really did not want to do. Day and night I badgered that sweet man until he finally relented, with one substantial condition: He wanted a ten percent down payment. Of course, we didn't have that kind of money. I was bemoaning my situation to a close friend when he surprised me. He had just received a payment from a family trust that was virtually equal to the amount I needed for the property. He lent me the money, and I bought the site on which Canine Assistants still stands.

So I had a place but I didn't yet have the money necessary to run a not-for-profit organization that wasn't going to charge anything for the services it provided (which is still the way Canine Assistants operates). I developed a business plan to open a boarding kennel in order to pay the bills as we got Canine Assistants up and running. As the "new kid on the block," I primarily got the dogs (and owners) that no veterinary clinic or established kennel wanted. Among our first guests were a dog who bit everyone and needed to wear a diaper, several dogs that chewed and swallowed chain-link fencing as if it were treats, multiple dogs who could escape from even the tallest fences, and countless dogs who enjoyed vocalizing day and night. And let me tell you, the dogs were the easy part of the job.

I had one owner who insisted on singing her dog, Mabel, to sleep over the phone each night at midnight. That wouldn't have been so bad except the lady was something of a drinker and would often lose her place and have to start her song over again and again before reaching the end. Sometimes, Mabel was on the phone for nearly an hour as I held the receiver to her ear. Those were long nights, but we probably would have been awake anyway. While the kennels were in portable buildings about two hundred feet from our house, complaints (understandable) from the neighbors about barking meant that I had to keep some of the loudest dogs in our basement. That did nothing to stop the barking. It just meant that only Mom and I, not the neighbors, could hear. We were tired people in those days.

Though money was still tight, it wasn't long before I was using the majority of the kennel space for service dogs. The response I had gotten from people who needed help was overwhelming. By November 1991, Canine Assistants had received its nonprofit status from the IRS, allowing contributions to be tax deductible. Before my first brochures were back from the printers, I had seventeen letters of application. Reading the stories of the people who applied made me realize how badly an organization that provided service dogs was needed. One letter was from a thirty-year-old woman who was asking for an assistance dog so she would not have to move into a nursing home. Another was from a young man who had muscular dystrophy and wanted a dog so he could fulfill his dream of going to college. The letter that touched me the most was from the mother of a little boy with cerebral palsy. She wrote that her son had no friends because he couldn't keep up with the other kids his age; a dog would give him some independence and keep him from being alone. All these years later I remember a quote from the mother's letter: "What is, after all, more natural and normal than a boy and his dog?"

Money was coming in, but very slowly and in small amounts. Mom and I made a combined total of $100 a week. We learned creative ways to survive. Canine Assistants recruited volunteers to do a majority of the work around the facility and to help with training. Date nights were great because they meant that someone else was paying for dinner. I would order an enormous amount of food and then eat about half, so that I could take the rest home for Mom. For clothes, we took on volunteers with good fashion sense and a willingness to "hand-me-down" in our direction. Somehow it all worked.

When we started, we adopted all of our dogs from shelters and rescue groups. In the years since Dad died, I'd spent much of my time reading about dogs, working in veterinary clinics, and watching classes given by local trainers. I felt confident that shelter dogs could be taught the skills necessary to be an assistance animal, and I was bound and determined to prove it. While our need for multiple dogs has led us to use both a breeding and rescue program, I remain a believer in adopting whenever possible. The breeds best suited to be assistance dogs are golden retrievers and Labs (or mixes thereof), because they have the right temperament, the natural inclination to retrieve, and an inviting public persona.

Sometimes adoption didn't go exactly as planned. Remember my sweet close friend who had helped me purchase the property? One day I asked him to go to the animal shelter to pick up a young dog I had tested earlier in the week. "This dog seems a little older than eighteen months," he said, after pulling into the driveway. That was an understatement. When the bony creature limped slowly from the backseat, it was obvious he was not the dog I had selected. His muzzle was completely gray and he was virtually toothless, but at least he was a golden retriever. We named him Old Fellow. Years later, my friend told me that the dog I asked him to pick up had already been adopted and that he just couldn't leave Old Fellow at the shelter to die.

One hot July morning, I went to the shelter looking for appropriate dogs for the program. I can still remember everything about that day: the awful stench—even worse than the usual shelter smell—the piercing barking and howling that resounded off the cinder-block walls, the cages stacked one atop the next, and the two big pens in the back jammed with beautiful creatures, males on the left, females on the right. As I approached the pen on the left, I noticed a dog lying on his side near the back wall. His skin was raw with open sores that oozed from infection. His emaciated frame made his eyes appear enormous. Clearly, he was not a good candidate for the program. So what did I do? I adopted him on the spot, of course. I named him Nicholas, Nick for short. Though later in his life Nick was to be described by Tom Brokaw as "a big, beautiful golden retriever," on this day he was a sorry example of the breed.

Nick was allergic to the cleanser used by the shelter, which had made his skin almost melt off his body. After only a few days at Canine Assistants, he began to heal and grew the most beautiful coat, thick and wavy and almost white. He was eight months old at the time I adopted him. Good food put weight on him, and he quickly became a seriously handsome dog. He was affectionate with adults and children alike. Nick was perfect for the program except

for one small flaw: He hated most other dogs, though that did improve some with age. The shelter staff told me that the other males
had regularly attacked him and as a consequence he developed an
aggression toward other dogs. In any case, we couldn't take the
chance that Nick would behave inappropriately with another dog
while tied to a recipient's wheelchair, so I decided to make him our
"spokesdog." It was a perfect fit. People were instantly attracted to
his good looks and amazing personality. He did such a wonderful
job of traveling with me to promote the program that I always think
of Canine Assistants as "The House That Nick Built."

Nick's influence reached beyond Canine Assistants. In fact, he was
the reason I met my husband. An insurance company interested in
working with veterinarians had asked Nick and me to be their
guests at a convention on Jekyll Island, Georgia. As always, Nicholas
was a tremendous draw. He was extremely smart and could bark out
the solutions to math problems, answer "yes" or "no" questions, and
generally woo the crowd for hours on end. During the convention,
one man decided it would be amusing to chase Nick around with a
cookie jar shaped like a cat that meowed when opened. Nick was
not at all amused by this and was starting to get a little freaked.
Fortunately, a young man who had noticed the teasing stepped in
between Nick and the dreaded cookie jar. He saw that we were in
distress and came to help. The man's name was Kent Bruner, and he
was so good-looking that I think I stared more than spoke when we
first met.

Kent, a veterinarian originally from Oklahoma, was working for
a veterinary pharmaceutical company. He was based in Atlanta and
lived not too far from Canine Assistants. He said that he missed
hands-on veterinary work and wanted to volunteer his services.
Veterinary care was a significant expense for us, so his offer was met
with swift and grateful acceptance. That he was handsome, charming, kind, and brilliant was, at that time, just a bonus. On his first volunteer visit, Kent made an amazing diagnosis that announced him
immediately as a gifted veterinarian. My own dog, a sweet golden

retriever named Samantha, had been eating poorly and not feeling well for some time. Although I had taken her to several vets, no one had yet been able to determine what was wrong. I asked Kent to examine her. As he tenderly ran his hands along her stomach, a look of agony came over his face. His diagnosis: Samantha had multiple tumors in her abdomen. An ultrasound confirmed that Kent was correct. The news was devastating. I was stunned that no fewer than three other veterinarians had palpated Samantha's belly repeatedly and hadn't felt what Kent did within seconds.

On his second visit, I handed him a pager so we could get in touch anytime we needed him. He was already working six-day weeks, traveling on most of those, but I couldn't afford to let that bother me—I just made sure his pager would work anywhere in the country. A few years down the road, I realized I needed him personally as much as the program needed him professionally.

It was Nick who was with me the morning I found that Mom had died peacefully in her sleep from a heart attack. Having gone through all that we had together, Mom and I were bound with a closeness difficult to describe. I couldn't imagine life without her; it didn't seem possible. My siblings were equally devastated, of course, but for all our grief, I daresay Nick was every bit as affected. Nick loved my mother with every fiber of his being, and he grieved desperately for her. For days he refused to let go of her pocketbook, even carrying it in his mouth to her funeral. Without Nick, I am not sure I would have survived my mother's death. I believe the feeling for Nick was the same.

It was Nick who helped me get ready for my wedding. Kent and I had planned to get married in April, but, after Mom died, we decided to move the wedding up. My brother, my two sisters, and several wonderful friends helped me plan the small ceremony. It was good for all of us, serving as a kind of reaffirmation of life. I had kept my dad's wedding ring on a chain around my neck since his death, as a remembrance of him and as a good-luck charm. I never took it off until my wedding day, when, surrounded by family and friends, I

slipped it onto Kent's ring finger. We had done a great job of planning, and all the important people in my life were there. But with all
the hurried-up planning for the wedding, I had forgotten to ask
anyone to stay with me the night before the ceremony at the house
Mom and I had shared. While that night was a happy time, full of
excitement and anticipation, I cannot imagine how lonely it would
have been had Nick not been there.

It was Nick who consoled me after Nanny's death. Shortly after
we got married, Kent and I moved Nanny into one of the small
houses on the Canine Assistants' property. We all felt the need to
kind of "circle the wagons" after Mom's death, wanting to be as
close to one another as possible. Nanny's daughter, Vicky, worked for
a dentist in Atlanta, and Nanny went down to stay with her on the
weekends. Vicky and I have always loved each other like sisters and
never minded sharing custody of Nanny.

One day Nanny called from her house next door. She was worried that the shrimp she had just eaten for dinner was bad. She was
vomiting and feeling lousy, and her condition continued to get
worse. We took her to a local hospital emergency room and discovered that she was having a heart attack. The doctors began treatment
immediately and Nanny quickly improved. I called Vicky, telling her
how much better Nanny seemed and that there was no need for her
to come to the hospital. I was certain Nanny would be fine, but I
was wrong. Thirty minutes later she had massive, fatal bleeding in
her brain from the drugs that she had been given for her heart. In
retrospect, the doctor thought that she might have had a prior, un-
diagnosed stroke, causing a weak spot in her brain.

Nick spent many days with his head on my shoulder as I lay sobbing in my bed. Finally, he moved his head from my shoulder to my
belly, reminding me that I had to move on. I was pregnant.

It was Nick to whom, six months later, I brought home my son,
Chase. I was terrified that Nick would be jealous of him. He wasn't.
Nick was instantly enamored of Chase and fiercely protective of
him, often giving me disapproving looks when Chase was crying. At
least Nick let me near him; most others were not so lucky. A friend
came to visit two weeks after Chase was born, and every time the

woman approached the baby, Nick growled. It was just a low, throaty little noise, but it was intimidating enough that the woman decided not to hold Chase. Bless her heart, she was incredibly annoying that day. She wouldn't leave, following me into my bedroom, where she talked through two of Chase's feedings and his afternoon nap. I was bleary-eyed and trying desperately to think of a nice way to ask her to leave when Nick, sensing my frustration, came out from under the bed and moved toward her, growling and barking. "So sorry," I said, "but you'd better go. It's not like him to act this way!" After the poor, frazzled woman fled, Nick jumped up on the bed, gave me a kiss, and went back to sleep.

It was Nick who first helped me realize that our training and handling methods might need to change. When the program started, I'd hired a trainer, with a great reputation and a willingness to work for little money, to instruct our assistance dogs. Though our trainer used techniques that were well accepted at the time, some of the dogs, especially Nick, did not do well with this methodology. The trainer relied heavily on negative-reinforcement techniques, such as leash corrections, choke-chain collars, and ear pinching. I taught those dogs that did not work well with her. We nicknamed my string of dogs the "special students," and they were indeed special. These incredible dogs did not turn out to be so much my students as they were my teachers. I had grown up riding horses, and I decided to apply the more positive approach I had always used with them. I quickly saw how effective enthusiastic praise and treat rewards were in training. Nick was at the top of the class, and I used him to further improve my positive-reinforcement methodology.

Since I used no force whatsoever, my special dogs quickly developed a sense of trust and a willingness to work. I used a rawhide chew rather than a traditional wooden dumbbell to teach retrieving; I used peanut butter on a wooden spoon to reinforce heeling; and I used Cheez Whiz to encourage tugging open doors and drawers. My group ended up being perfect partners for people with disabilities. Assistance dogs must be especially sensitive and responsive, and once trained, they need to help their human partners by doing a variety of physical tasks while being emotionally in tune enough with their partners to recognize if anything is wrong. The vast majority of recipients cannot physically dominate their dogs, so the dogs must comply out of devotion rather than from fear or force. The dogs I have trained using only positive motivation trust people completely.

I would like to tell you that right then and there I insisted that all of our dogs be handled in this kinder way. It should have been the obvious progression, but sadly that was not the case. It is something that haunts me still, but at the time I did not have the confidence or maturity to trust my instincts and separate from the traditional training methodology. For me, there was no sudden shift from physical corrections to the positive-only approach; rather, it was a slow evolution with many mistakes along the way.

Watching the dogs we trained at Canine Assistants change people's lives certainly helped my evolutionary process. It is difficult to be harsh with a dog who is so willing to help someone else. Working with children and adults who have mobility difficulties or seizure conditions, these incredible dogs learn to do a variety of tasks, such as turning lights on and off, opening and closing doors, pushing buttons, picking up dropped objects, and running for help in an emergency. They transform lives with their constant companionship and unconditional love in ways that no human can equal. I have witnessed hundreds of remarkable relationships between dogs and people. One in particular stands out for me.

A young mother approached me during a two-week training camp at Canine Assistants, with tears streaming down her face. She wanted to warn me that her eight-year-old son, who was facing his sixth surgery to correct a spinal-column deformity, might not want to take home a dog. Her son had recently told her that he was sorry but he just couldn't keep trying and that he was ready to go to heaven and be with God. Imagine how difficult it must have been to hear those words from her child. In an effort to give him hope, she had convinced him to come to Canine Assistants to at least "meet" the dogs. Her son had reluctantly agreed. On the third day of training camp, we matched the dogs with their new recipients. Surprisingly, the boy appeared quite happy with his dog, but the following morning, his mother again came to me crying. My heart sank. I was afraid she was going to tell me that her son didn't want his dog. "Last night," she said, "I asked my son if he still wanted to go on to heaven." His reply: "Oh, no, Mom! I can't go now. I can't leave my dog. He needs me."

Maybe we can't say the dog saved his life, but we can certainly say he rescued the boy's desire to live. Good work for an eighteen-month-old golden retriever puppy! I cannot imagine a situation in which this dog would deserve to have his ears pinched or his collar yanked or his trust violated in any way.

What changed my methodology the most was my increased understanding of dogs and their perspective of the world we share. My approach to handling changed as my understanding of dogs grew, until one day I realized that it was morally wrong to treat dogs with anything other than patience, understanding, and kindness. I have come to appreciate that dogs are capable of deep feeling, that they have individual personalities and intellectual capacities, extraordinary at times. Most of all I have learned that, beyond all other species, dogs have evolved to be our partners, protectors, and helpmates.

CHAPTER TWO

When Dogs Began

When I was four, a little girl from nursery school invited me to her house to play. It was my very first playdate. When Mom drove me to the girl's house, we pulled up in front of a nice two-story residence. Before we could get out of the car, a man came running out and explained that this wasn't the main house but rather the gatehouse. The "big house," as he called it, was another mile up the drive. And it *was* enormous, with a huge swimming pool, several tennis courts, an indoor bowling alley, a giant playhouse, and a barn full of ponies. As Mom waved good-bye, promising to return in a few hours, she despaired that she would ever get me to leave that wonderland. She recalled being utterly shocked that, not only did I go home willingly, once in the car I burst into tears, sobbing out how sad I felt that my friend had to live in such a horrible place.

"Horrible?" Mom said. "They have everything a little girl could possibly want there."

"No, Mama, they don't," I wailed. "They aren't allowed to have dogs."

As a child, I could not imagine a fate worse than living without a dog. As an adult, I realize that there are fates far worse for some than living without a dog, but I am still hard-pressed to list many applicable to my own life. My mom used to say that my love of dogs seemed to have been genetically encoded in me. My research into the history of the relationship between man and dog suggests that my mom may well have been right.

Shortly before Dad died in 1980, he showed me an article he'd come across that described an archaeological discovery made by Simon Davis and François Valla. The two had recently unearthed an ancient burial site in northern Israel dating back to 9350 B.C., which contained both human and animal remains. An elderly woman shared her grave with the remains of a young dog. Even more interesting was the unique positioning of the two skeletons. Davis and Valla found the two bodies close together, with the old woman's hand positioned over the body of the puppy in a gesture of affection. I was enchanted by the thought that people had lived with and loved dogs for a remarkably long time. I began to research the evolution of man's relationship to dogs.

Darwin and many other scientists theorized, given the enormous diversity of dog breeds, that the dog must have had multiple wild ancestors. Wolves, jackals, and coyotes were all thought to be progenitors of today's modern dogs. However, in 1997, a group of international scientists led by Robert Wayne at the University of California–Los Angeles studied the genetic makeup of domesticated dogs, wolves, jackals, and coyotes. The results proved unequivocally that our dogs have but one wild ancestor—the wolf. From a personal standpoint, I liked that news. I'm sure jackals and coyotes are lovable creatures to those who know them, but I myself do not know a single jackal or coyote—though I did once see a coyote crossing the road near my house, with what I believed to be the neighbor's rooster in his mouth. I do, however, know a few wolves, and I much prefer to think of my noble dogs as the progeny of these beautiful and intelligent creatures.

Our natural attraction to dogs may well have begun with wolves. When you think about it, humans and wolves are surprisingly similar in many ways. We are both species who live in groups based on family units. The fathers and mothers in both species are afforded great respect, and these parents develop a relationship with every other member in their group. The communal raising of children is found in wolves and humans. Both species use courtship as a way of choosing a mate. In wolves, the courtship period is typically at least a year in length; often, mating doesn't enter into the relationship until even later. Young adult wolves often set out from the group they were raised in to begin a family of their own.

Humans and wolves must both function as a team in order to survive and prosper. Mammals such as elephants and chimpanzees are gatherers rather than hunters. Gathering can be done individually. Neither wolves nor early humans were strong enough to overcome large prey or fast enough to catch elusive prey on their own, so both species needed the cooperation of a group in order to succeed. Cooperation requires communication. Each member of the group must be able to understand the others. Both species excel at communication. Teamwork also requires that each member be willing to put the needs of the team above their own, another trait wolves and humans share.

Bonding is critical to the survival of any group. Corporate managers invest substantial sums to have their employees participate in team-building exercises. Games and challenges are used as tools to teach the need for members to trust and rely upon one another. Games are an essential part of the bonding process. Adult wolves, too, use play as a way to bond with friends and family. They engage in energetic games of tag, they love to pounce on and wrestle with one another, and at times puppies are even allowed to "pin" the grown-ups.

Given all the similarities between humans and wolves, it seems inevitable that we would be attracted to one another. Indeed, it seems that our attraction was the very basis for the development of the species we call dogs.

Just when did wolves evolve into dogs? There are two primary theories. For many years, evolutionary archaeologists believed that dogs came into being between 12,000 and 14,000 years ago. However, DNA evidence generated by Robert Wayne and Charles Vila of

UCLA in 1997 suggests that wolves evolved into dogs much earlier—135,000 years ago or more. The discrepancy depends upon the interpretation of fossil and DNA evidence.

Dog skeletons are easily distinguished from those of wolves, since dogs have smaller skulls and teeth. All experts agree that dogs have existed for at least 12,000 to 14,000 years, based on ample evidence of fossils found in or near human settlements. Mankind was then on the verge of domesticating sheep and cattle and learning to grow crops such as wheat, maize, and rice. People lived in larger groups, and dogs would have been a great help with communal tasks such as hunting and guarding.

Wayne and Vila's earlier domestication date is controversial. Critics maintain that the 135,000-year-old fossils look structurally akin to the wolf and could not have come from dogs. Supporters of the Wayne-Vila theory respond to this criticism by saying that early dogs still looked like wolves, they just *behaved* differently. Does it matter which date is correct? It does to us dog lovers. If, indeed, dogs have been around for 135,000 years, this would suggest that rather than humans helping with the evolution of dogs, the two species may have co-evolved or influenced the evolution of each other.

Homo sapiens had just evolved from *Homo erectus* at that point. People were still primitive, having mastered fire and the use of simple tools as well as building basic structures and sewing clothing from hides. Beyond that, however, these early *Homo sapiens* did not much resemble modern humans. Civilization was a long way off; *Homo sapiens* had only a rudimentary grasp of communal living. Wolves, on the other hand, seem to have always excelled at living and working in harmony. It could well be that humans owe an important part of our own development to watching, interacting with, and emulating canids, the species group that includes both wolves and dogs.

Just as there are two primary theories regarding *when* wolves evolved into dogs, there are two primary theories regarding *how* wolves evolved into dogs. Some researchers believe that humans bred wolves in such a way as to create dogs. This type of species manipulation is known as artificial selection. Others think that some wolves decided to stay close to humans and that those wolves, over generations, evolved into dogs. This is known as natural selection.

When I was first learning to talk, my parents had a running wager as to whether "Mama" or "Dada" would be the first recognizable word I said. One evening they were both playing with me on the floor. "D-d-d," I said, poking my chubby little finger out. "Yes!" my dad shouted in excited encouragement. But as he reached his arms out to hug me, I moved past him, heading straight for our dog and finishing the word with "ahgg." Somehow, I don't believe it surprised either of them that my first word was "dog." Our family pet (a poodle) had always been my favorite toy.

In his book *Biophilia,* Edward O. Wilson explains his belief that we are born programmed to look at and interact with the living things around us. Dogs, he believes, are particularly attractive to humans because of their constant presence and their similar behaviors, such as group living, mutual cooperation, game playing, and reciprocated affection.

It is possible that people could have adopted wolf puppies and bred them in such a manner that the entity would be considered a new species. In 1958, a Russian geneticist named Dmitry Belyaev began to selectively breed foxes in Siberia. Some claim that Belyaev was working for the fur industry, trying to create a fox breed that could be more easily handled by people. He began his study with foxes that were the least likely to run from humans. After eighteen generations, he finally had foxes with big eyes and gentle expressions that would follow him around and cuddle with him like puppies. They were also useless to the fur trade, because most had multicolored coats rather than the prized sleek reddish coats of wild foxes. It turns out the same gene that controls fear in animals also controls coat color. Lucky for those foxes.

Given Belyaev's results, it is conceivable that people could have taken wolf pups to hand-raise and then bred the friendliest of the lot in order to create the domestic dog. However, it took Belyaev eighteen generations to breed naturally tame foxes. Since wolves mature at around the age of two and have only one litter a year, it would have taken early man at least thirty-six years of careful, deliberate breeding, and that's if everything went well at each breeding and birthing. Additionally, even so-called "tame" wolves are extremely difficult to manage and potentially very dangerous to humans. I have had several opportunities to work with these magnificent creatures, and they are nothing like dogs. Even captive wolves are serious hunters and have absolutely no interest in the antics of humans, unless those antics result in the wolves getting food. They are extremely quick to take offense when humans mistakenly violate their code of behavior by looking them in the eye too long or by approaching them head-on rather than from the side. Those human offenders are usually corrected with multiple "strikes," or quick bites. Even wolves raised by humans remain wild animals in most senses of the word. Combine the inherent difficulties and risks involved in breeding wolves with the fact that early man could not have known the potential of such an experiment, and this theory does not quite hold up.

It seems to me much more plausible that wolves themselves began their own domestication and that humans supported the effort. Wolves who began hanging around human settlements in order to eat discarded scraps or unattended food stashes were likely bolder wolves, less afraid of being in close proximity to humans. These braver wolves had stumbled onto a food source far more reliable than prey hunting—people. Additionally, it seems probable that many of the wolves who first approached human settlements were not part of a pack. Living with a group—even humans, and even on their outskirts—was safer than going it alone. The food, water, and safety provided to wolves who stayed close to human settlements meant their puppies were more likely to survive into adulthood.

Humans must have recognized that wolves, as they evolved into dogs, had innate characteristics that would be helpful in the people's daily lives. For one thing, the animals were pleased to consume human garbage and other unspeakable waste products, leaving settlements cleaner. Early dogs could help with hunting and, as they had a higher body temperature than humans, could be used for warmth. Dogs would also guard territory and resources, alerting people to the presence of danger and defending the encampment.

Ultimately, the changes in wolves would have been much like the changes in Belyaev's foxes—softer eyes, less wild behavior, and substantially less aggression. Their puppies would have been playful, sweet natured, and gentle. Indeed, those puppylike characteristics would have been retained into adulthood, a process called neoteny. At this point, humans began to contribute to the development of the species, taking these new creatures into their homes and breeding them for specific traits.

Ever since dogs came into being, when man has been in need, the dog has come to the rescue. I am fortunate enough to see it every single day with the dogs at Canine Assistants, who give themselves without hesitation to help those who need them.

Lindsay, a golden retriever, lives with an older woman, Carol, who has epilepsy. From the time the two first met at Canine Assistants, Lindsay has known when Carol is going to have a seizure. As soon as she realizes a seizure is impending, Lindsay alerts Carol by tugging gently on her sleeve and whining softly. Once Carol is safely situated, Lindsay goes into the bedroom, retrieves the handheld phone, and takes it to Carol should she need to call for help. Then Lindsay goes back into the bedroom, tugs open a bedside table drawer, grabs Carol's post-seizure medicine, and delivers it. Next Lindsay goes to the kitchen, tugs open the refrigerator, gets a bottle of water, closes the refrigerator door, and takes the water to Carol so she can swallow her medicine. If Lindsay is particularly concerned about Carol, she may push a button to alert apartment management to the situation. Finally, Lindsay lies down next to Carol and waits it out.

One day, Nick and I were visiting an Atlanta pediatric hospital. Nick was dressed in his doctor's uniform, complete with scrub top, stethoscope, pager, and black bag. Many of the children at the hospital had already met my big golden retriever, and they had nicknamed him Dr. Nick. As we were about to leave the cancer unit, a nurse ran up to ask if we had time to visit one more child.

The nurse explained that the fifteen-year-old boy had recently

lost his leg to cancer and wasn't doing well emotionally or psycho-
logically. Since his surgery, he had lost the will to fight. He rarely ate;
he didn't cry or rant or scream about the unfairness of life or do any
of the things considered "healthy" for a child in his situation. The
nurse had little hope that we could get through to the boy, but she
asked that we try.

I remember pushing open the door to his room and seeing a
very handsome, very bald young man propped up in the bed. The
deep circles under his eyes made him seem so old. He was staring
blankly at a get-well card taped to his wall and gave me only a brief
glance as we entered. After a few seconds, he seemed to catch sight
of Dr. Nick for the first time and smiled faintly. Without waiting for
my direction, Nick dropped his black bag and jumped onto the bed.
The boy's frail arms came up and wrapped tightly around Nick's
neck, and he buried his head into the thick fur as Nick leaned back
against him. The young man began to sob. He cried for a long time,
until there was no crying left in him, and then he began to talk to
Nick. It was as if they were alone in the room. He told Nick about
his pain and fear until he had completely exhausted himself. As we
left, I promised to bring Nick back to visit soon.

The nurse called the following morning. The boy was eating and
talking—talking mostly about Dr. Nick. He was telling everyone
who would listen how much he would love to have a dog like Nick.
Dr. Nick and I visited several times a week, and each time this young
man clung a little longer and a little harder to Nick. And each time
it became more difficult not to tell the boy of my surprise for him.
I was training a golden retriever, his own Nick. Before long, the day
came and the young man met his big dog. He assured me countless
times that it was the best day of his life.

There weren't many days left in that precious boy's life. Those he
did have were filled with the love of a wonderful dog. When the boy
died, he died with his arms wrapped around a big golden retriever
of his own.

The greater the need, the more the dogs are willing and able to
do. There are countless examples of the heroic, selfless behavior of
dogs, but here are two from recent times.

During the memorial for those killed in the 1995 Oklahoma City bombing, all the rescue workers were deservedly greeted with great applause, but it wasn't until the search-and-rescue dogs that had worked the site entered the room that the crowd leapt to its feet. The cheering could be heard from blocks away. Most were responding to a photograph that had been published of a golden retriever named Aspen, wearing her orange vest and being held in the arms of her human partner, Skip Fernandez. In the photo, Fernandez appears exhausted, but it is the golden whose image is truly haunting. Fernandez is quoted as having said, "When she finds live people, she barks. When she finds bodies, she whines. She has been doing a lot of whining." The pain underlying those whines is visible on Aspen's beautiful face. The photograph is unquestionably a picture of shared agony, but beyond the agony is the clear message that man does not face the pain alone.

Omar Eduardo Rivera did not face the pain of September 11, 2001, alone. His guide dog, Dorado, would not let him. Rivera was in his office on the seventy-first floor of the World Trade Center's North Tower when the hijacked airliner hit the building some twenty-five stories above him. Amid the chaos that ensued, Mr. Rivera decided his plight was hopeless but wanted to give Dorado a chance to survive. With that in mind, Rivera unclipped Dorado's leash and told him to run. Dorado did go, briefly. Within minutes, Rivera felt Dorado's muzzle. The dog refused to leave without him. With Dorado leading, they both made it safely down seventy-one floors and out onto the sidewalk.

History would have been rewritten many times were it not for dogs—in large public moments as well as small personal ones. Given the importance of the relationship, it is surprising that humans still understand very little about dogs. How strongly are our dogs influenced by their wolf ancestry and what exactly is that heritage? How much can we expect them to be like a child or child substitute? Are they "man's best friend" or merely a parasitic species living off the largesse of humankind? While aspects of these questions will remain debated for many years, we know enough to formulate some reasonable answers.

CHAPTER THREE

Children in Wolves' Clothing

Back in the early days of Canine Assistants, a woman who worked with my mom asked us to keep her dog, a malamute named Kee, while she was traveling. Kee was a loving, friendly dog who bore an uncanny resemblance to her wolf ancestors. Nick was standing beside me at the window as Kee and her mom came through our front gate and down the driveway toward the house. For a brief moment, Nick froze, then he took off at full speed for the bedroom. Our wooden floors wouldn't allow him to get solid traction, and he looked a little like Scooby-Doo running from a ghost, legs spinning but going nowhere. Finally, he made it to the bedroom and dove headfirst under the bed, something I'd never seen Nick do. He paused momentarily as if contemplating the circumstances, jumped out again, grabbed my shirtsleeve, and began pulling me—I needed to be safely under the bed with him.

It took an hour for Nick to make his way out to meet Kee. Once he had smelled her thoroughly, he relaxed and the two became great playmates. Nick was a very forward dog who had never before shown that kind of fear. Perhaps Nick thought Kee was a wolf. From time to time people mistook the big malamute for one. Then again, some people seem to think all dogs are just wolves in poodle clothing.

How much are dogs like wolves? Or are they more like human children? Nothing in the animal world is more intensely debated today than how we should view and treat our dogs. Beliefs are often strongly held and poles apart.

Lupomorphism is the belief that dogs are much like wolves and that the behavior of the wolf pack should be our primary guide in handling our dogs. Dogs, however, evolved from wolves long ago, and once evolution has occurred, it is no longer possible to characterize a species—or a subspecies, as dogs are now considered—exactly as their genetic ancestors. There are a number of physical differences that distinguish dogs from wolves, including smaller skulls and smaller, more-rounded teeth. Also, dogs are behaviorally and emotionally different from wolves. They are more willing to work with people and are much better at reading human body language. While there are obvious similarities, the differences between wolves and dogs are substantial.

Additionally, the tendency to misinterpret wolf behavior through untrained human eyes is almost unavoidable, leading to potentially disastrous results when those misinterpretations are applied to our dogs. Some animal behaviorists and dog trainers believe that studies of wolves dictate that dogs should be dominated, physically and emotionally, so that they will acknowledge the human as the alpha "pack leader." However, the consensus among wolf researchers is that bullying is *not* how alpha wolves achieve and maintain their power status. Alpha wolves in the wild are often the biological parents of the other pack members and as such are instinctively treated with respect. Some watch the behavior patterns of captive wolves, not wolves in the wild, to formulate their methods of dog handling. Captive wolf packs are usually "bastardized" families, where there isn't a clear mother, father, or sibling structure. Therefore, wolves that would like to assume the alpha roles often have to fight viciously to achieve and maintain power. Additionally, the position and status of older and younger siblings isn't clearly defined in most captive packs.

In the wild, mother and father wolves tend to be benevolent leaders. A friend recently told me a story about a researcher who wanted to study the feeding habits of wolves in the wild—specifically, who would eat first and who would eat last. The researcher threw out four chickens for the pack and watched. The alpha male picked up the first chicken and took it to a female who was caring for young pups. The second chicken went to the teenagers and older pups. The third went to the alpha female, and the alpha male ate the last chicken. While the alpha could eat first, as no one would stop him, he had no need to show dominance. This contradicts fashionable training advice that owners should always eat before feeding their dogs so that leadership is clearly defined. It also debunks the idea of having to roll your dog onto his back, put your hand across his throat, and stare menacingly to prove you are the lead wolf, a behavior also advocated by some popular trainers.

Such advice is absurd. The dominance model for dog training is based on faulty science and is in fact dangerous for our dogs. I have witnessed and heard of acts of cruelty perpetrated in an effort to "establish dominance." It is time to let go of the whole "alpha" concept. Your dog already knows you aren't a wolf or another dog. Dogs are pretty sharp that way. You are already the boss in your dog's eyes. You get to do whatever you want, the true definition of alpha. You control the food and the toys. You provide shelter and security. Anyway, if you want your dog to adapt to living in human society, why would you try to act like a dog—or, worse, like a wolf?

People are being told that it is not only okay to treat their dogs without respect, it is necessary for a good relationship. Just the opposite is true. Your dog deserves your respect, and giving him that respect is the only way to have a healthy, happy relationship.

There are without question similarities between dogs and wolves that deserve our attention, since they are important to understanding and appreciating the whole dog. After all, comprehending the behavioral traits shared by all canids makes life with our dogs easier.

Dogs and wolves both practice territorial and resource guarding. Most pet dogs seem to feel the need to guard their humans. Why? While humans do provide food, shelter, and an overall sense of security, a dog must find us ill-equipped for the job of alerting to potential intruders. We can't see movement well, we can barely smell, and we're nearly deaf compared to dogs. The first to recognize danger, our dogs are the first to alert the others and the first to stage a defense. Because the safety of the group is paramount to all canids, our dogs feel the need to defend us.

This tendency, if handled incorrectly, can at times cause your sweet Fluffy to bark like Cujo. Take a simple visit from Grandpa. As he barges into your house, Fluffy goes off. There's Fluffy just doing her job as nature intended by howling and growling (unfortunately, at Gramps), and what do you, her fearless leader, do? You fuss at her for barking and, since she doesn't speak Human, she thinks you are freaked out about Grandpa too. Imagine if you felt afraid of something and the person you trusted most started to speak in an unpleasant tone in a language you couldn't understand? Wouldn't you likely think he was also afraid of the intruder?

Nick always enjoyed having people visit our house. We frequently had volunteers wandering in to use the kitchen or do kennel laundry. Nick welcomed them all—until, that is, we began to deliver puppies in our laundry room. Once that first puppy was born, Nick became a ferocious guard dog, refusing to allow anyone but family and a few close friends access to that part of the house. When each litter of puppies reached four weeks of age—about the time they began to eat solid food—he would relax and once again welcome all human visitors. However, Nick continued to keep other dogs away until the puppies had left the house altogether.

So what about your dog guarding you from other dogs? Consider this scenario: While walking your dog, you pass a man peacefully walking his dog. Your dog begins to bark as if the sight of the other dog upsets him. What do you do? You begin to pull on your dog's collar in preparation for trouble. You fuss at your dog for barking. Your body language signals fear. What have you accomplished? Well, you probably just started a dogfight!

Think about your dog's perception of you, his leader, and your reaction to his barking. Your words are angry and fearful. He does not understand your literal words, just your tone. You telegraph stress when you choke up on the leash, not to mention probably causing your dog some physical discomfort. Your body language screams fear. Your dog thinks you are terrified of the approaching pair. In an effort to protect you both, your dog becomes more aggressive. You respond with more fear. Bada boom—*dogfight!*

Dogs can perceive threats from any variation in their normal environment, routine, or circumstances. Additionally, they remember past stresses, both emotional and physical, and may respond to such memories. When I first adopted Nick from the shelter, he would bark ferociously whenever he saw men with beards, clearly indicating a negative history. Any beard more than scruff would send him into hysterics. In an effort to ease Nick's concern, I recruited every bearded man I knew. Then I pulled out my secret weapon: a big bag of chewy treats. I had the men parade past Nick and me as we walked down the street. When Nick would start barking, I'd open the bag of treats and, as he stopped for a split second to smell the goodies, I'd break off a piece, feed it to him, and tell him he was a good boy. As we approached the fifth bearded passerby, Nick skipped the barking altogether and starting nudging the bag for his treat. Smart boy. Nick showed a decided fondness for bearded men for the rest of his life, even though treats were rarely part of the equation after the first few days. Understanding what your dog is thinking and positively addressing the issue can correct whatever situation needs correcting.

Once I fed Nick a treat, I didn't try to pull it back out of his mouth. Our dogs are easier to handle than wolves when it comes to resource protecting, but it is a trait dogs and wolves do share. If you tried to take food or a toy from a wolf, it would attack you. It's interesting to note that possession is paramount to wolves. If a lower-ranking individual has a bone, more-dominant pack members will usually leave him alone. And if they don't, the wolf with the bone is likely to try to keep it even if it means growling at a parent. Most pet dogs will tolerate having food or toys taken from them by their owners, but that is not always a given, so approach with caution and be prepared to make a "trade" with your dog, if necessary.

Wolves and dogs are both hunters by nature and, as such, realize that hunting is a gamble. Success isn't guaranteed. My mom used to send me directly to the seafood shop whenever Dad left the house to go fishing, promising he was going to bring home our supper. Good thing she did. We would have gone hungry after many of Dad's fishing trips without store-bought fish. Fear of going hungry is deeply rooted within all true hunters. For our dogs, this fear is manifested in a very simple, totally predictable behavior: They eat whatever they can, whenever they can. Their genetic hardwiring constantly reminds dogs that they don't know for sure when food might again be available. I know many people who have been shocked that their dogs have climbed on the counter and eaten the food that was awaiting human consumption. This doesn't surprise me in the least. Nick once opened my refrigerator (my fault—I'd taught him to tug open doors) and helped himself to an entire Thanksgiving dinner. Of course, there are some exceptions. Dogs who don't seem to have much of a hunger drive may willingly leave food alone, but the majority of dogs operate under the fear of potential deprivation.

When I take service-dogs-in-training out into public, people often come up and tell me all about their own dogs. One day I had a young female golden at a local mall when a woman ran up and told me her dog looked just like mine. She went on to explain that her dog was so good that every night she'd leave dinner on the coffee table in their den and her dog wouldn't touch it. I couldn't quite imagine this behavior from a young retriever.

"What does she do if you leave food on the kitchen counters?" I asked.

"Oh, she isn't tall enough yet, but I am sure she wouldn't eat it. She just knows better," the woman replied. "We never even had to teach her."

Now I was thinking the dog either had no sense of smell, wasn't very food-driven (highly unlikely for a retriever), or was, for some reason, afraid of the table.

"Did she ever have anything bad happen to her when she got near the coffee table?" I asked.

"No, " the woman said quickly, then paused. "Except when she was younger, my husband would bump her on her nose when she would sniff things on the table. But nothing bad happened to her." Wow.

"Your dog is afraid of the coffee table," I told her. I suggested she be careful about leaving food in other places, because her dog would probably eat it.

"Don't be silly," the woman huffed. "My dog is smart enough to know better than to eat food that doesn't belong to her."

I have worried about that dog. I bet she grew enough to reach the kitchen counters and, at some point, wolfed down a honey-baked ham. The woman was most likely furious, assuming that her dog "knew better." Poor dog.

The woman and her husband had found one way to keep their dog from stealing food from the coffee table—they made her terrified to get near it. But I have an idea how to keep dogs from stealing food that is both easier and kinder. *Don't leave food out where your dog can reach it*. Problem solved.

Another characteristic shared by dogs and wolves is the tendency to use urine for purposes other than relieving a full bladder. As a matter of fact, peeing can accomplish a great deal in the world of canids. First, dogs use the scent of urine to mark territory and provide information, such as age and breeding readiness, to other dogs. You know how some dogs, mine included, sniff each bush and hydrant when taking a walk? We refer to that as "reading their pee-mail." Some unneutered male dogs may want to mark territory even in your home—just one of the many reasons it is a great idea to neuter (or spay) your dog.

Younger dogs will occasionally use urination in an effort to show submission to you or another dog. This behavior is most likely designed to indicate, "I'm just a baby," and probably stems from their newborn stage, when they could not urinate or defecate until their mothers had licked their urogenital area. This is true for both dogs and wolves. Dogs that urinate for this reason are attempting to acknowledge your leadership, not annoy you. Submissive urination is a behavior your dog will most likely grow out of, usually by about eighteen months of age at the very latest. Young dogs, especially females, don't have great muscle control. When they get excited, they simply can't hold their urine. Forgive her excitement. Ignoring the dog or punishing her, as some trainers recommend, is cruel, since this is something she cannot yet control.

Dogs and wolves want to keep their dens clean, but what constitutes the den to your dog is limited to the areas where you sleep and spend the most time, such as your family room. Dogs that run into seldom-used areas, such as the formal dining room or the living room, to relieve themselves believe that they are outside their den. Housebroken dogs who suddenly begin to eliminate inside may have a physical or emotional condition, such as infection, diabetes, or separation anxiety.

Wolves and dogs can throw up at will. In fact, this is how mother canids teach their puppies to eat solid food. Pups stimulate their mother to vomit by licking near her mouth. Dogs have kept this instinctual drive and, as a result, they tend to jump up uninvited to kiss and lick our faces. Since dogs—and puppies in particular—are programmed to receive information about appropriate conduct from their consorts and caregivers, the jumping—indeed, any undesirable behavior—can easily be channeled into a more acceptable one, with guidance and positive reinforcement.

Chewing is natural and necessary for both wolves and dogs, helping to keep jaws strong and teeth clean. Sometimes dogs will chew simply out of boredom. My godson, who is eight months old, seems to feel the same way. He, too, puts most everything he can reach into his mouth. This is not the only characteristic that children and dogs have in common.

Babymorphism is the view that dogs are much like very young children and should be treated as such. A study conducted at the University of Vienna and published in the American scientific journal *Current Biology* found that dogs have the approximate intellect of a fourteen-month-old child. Other research has estimated that dogs have varying levels of intelligence equivalent to children ranging in age from fourteen months to two years. So treating a dog as you might a human toddler makes some degree of sense. Dogs, like toddlers, are totally dependent upon us for survival. They have no ability to get their own meals; they cannot bathe themselves; they cannot go running loose through the neighborhood without facing significant danger.

We once had a woman come into Canine Assistants with a beautiful young black Lab. The woman explained that she and her husband had loved the dog like a child, until they had what she described as "a real child." Now, she claimed, they could no longer care for the dog and wanted us to take him. I was speechless. However, the volunteer standing with me was not. Very calmly, the volunteer asked, "Are you and your husband planning to have more than one child?"

The young woman replied, "We'd like to have at least two."

"Have you thought about how you will find a home for your first child once your second comes?" When the woman looked confused, the volunteer explained, "It seems you can love and care for only one being at a time, so I was wondering what you were planning to do with your firstborn when another child comes along."

Like young kids, dogs have the capacity to make you feel like the center of the universe, and, to a real extent, you are the center of their universe—loved to the point of worship. As a toddler, my son, Chase, always enjoyed going to day care. Yet when I would walk into the room to pick him up each afternoon, his face would instantly light up with pure joy. He would drop whatever he was doing and run toward me, his little legs moving as fast as they could. I was the heart of his world, and there was no better feeling. No drug known to man can produce such euphoria. And what does your dog do when he sees you? Greets you just like a toddler does, doesn't he? Our dogs never grow past the point of seeing us as their universe. Is it any wonder we adore them?

We buy them gifts, brush their teeth, comb their hair, and clean up after them. We hire dog-sitters or take them to day care. Some refer to their dogs as "kids" and themselves as "pet parents." So attached are we to our dogs that any divorce lawyer worth his or her salt is familiar with how local judges handle canine custody issues. For most judges today, that means deciding what is in the best interest of the dog. Dogs may be legally classified as property, but, fortunately, few treat them that way.

That said, the idea of treating dogs as children can lead you into the hazardous world of anthropomorphism. Dogs and humans are alike in many ways. So, to a modest extent, anthropomorphizing our pets can be valid. However, when comparing dogs and children, you must remember two things: First, if we can fairly compare dogs to humans in some ways, we can compare them only to young toddlers, with all the physical, emotional, and intellectual limits that suggests. Dogs do not understand the concept of social rules and so they, like young children, function best when redirected rather than corrected. Second, dogs and toddlers process many things quite differently, so there are times when anthropomorphism is incredibly unfair to your dog. Dogs and children are similar, not identical.

Nick and I were in the park one day when we passed a young woman walking her dalmatian. The woman had clearly obeyed the PLEASE CURB YOUR DOG sign, as she was carrying a plastic bag with evident distaste and moving quickly toward the trash can. The bag was filled with what can only be described as rainbow-colored poop. Seeing me looking at the bag, the young woman gave her dog a nasty glance and said that, though she had explained to her dog many times that crayons were not for eating, the dog persisted in consuming any her daughter left out. What made her think her dog could understand that concept? I asked pleasantly. She had recently read that dogs were as smart as sixteen-month-old children, and her child-care book noted that sixteen-month-olds could understand that crayons were for drawing, not for eating. The young woman felt sure her dog was "just trying to make her daughter mad."

No matter how many times you explain to your dog that crayons are for coloring, you will never come home to find that he has drawn you a lovely picture of the beach. Of course, your dog probably doesn't understand the word "crayon," much less how to properly use one. The failure to understand the many ways in which dogs and children differ places unrealistic demands on your dog.

In direct opposition to those who see dogs as virtually human, there are some researchers who theorize that they are nothing more than social parasites. They contend that dogs figured out how to make humans care for and love them but that dogs do not love us in return. Dogs have, in essence, hoodwinked humans into feeding and sheltering them for the many thousands of years of their existence. Can this be true? Wolves and early dogs gave more benefit *to* human society than they received *from* it. They ate garbage, alerted people to potential harm, and provided warmth in the cold. In exchange, they got food, water, and shelter, unless, of course, times were lean—then humans ate them and wore their skins.

Today, dogs herd for us, guide us, assist us, help police us, sniff out dangers, lower our blood pressure, and provide numerous other societal benefits. There are thousands of dogs whose physical assistance saves their owners far more than the dogs themselves cost in upkeep. I know hundreds of cases where people would have to be in state-run nursing homes were it not for the help of their dogs. Imagine how overcrowded the offices of psychotherapists would be were it not for the presence of dogs in our lives. For all they give, we provide for them—as long as it is convenient for us. They would have gotten a better deal living with chimpanzees. I'm sure the dogs themselves realize that, having undoubtedly spent a great deal of time assessing the cost-benefit analysis of their relationship with mankind.

"What?" you say. "Dogs don't have enough higher cognitive function to do cost-benefit analysis." Then they also don't have the cognitive capacity required to run the largest and longest-lasting con the world has ever known.

Even if you can accept that dogs are capable of running that kind of scam, then just how stupid are we? People spend many billions of dollars annually on their dogs. Is it feasible that we would do that if dogs gave us absolutely nothing in return? In any analysis of the relationship between humans and dogs, humans come out way ahead.

We know that dogs retain some of the characteristics of their wolf ancestors but that their very evolution itself means that they aren't exactly like wolves anymore. We know that dogs have similarities to children, yet we realize that dogs aren't merely little people in furry suits. And, despite the contention of some, dogs aren't social parasites. So how exactly can the relationship between dog and man be characterized? Just who are they to us?

Clyde Murphy, a Labrador retriever, was just two years old when he became a hero. He had graduated only months before and become a certified assistance dog to Pam, a quadriplegic woman dependent on a ventilator. Pam's daughter, Debbie, had just taken Clyde out for a walk when he suddenly began to pull her frantically toward the front door. Debbie tried to correct him, as she knew he wasn't supposed to pull on his leash. It didn't work. After she had done everything she could think of to make Clyde settle down, Debbie gave up and allowed him to return to the house. As Debbie opened the front door, she heard the noise her whole family dreaded. An alarm was sounding, signaling that Pam's tracheostomy tube had become disconnected from its outlet. Debbie ran to her mother's room and quickly reconnected the tube. Pam regained her air supply—and Clyde was a hero. A few minutes later, the young hero willingly went out for his walk, but he didn't wander far.

Though Clyde hadn't been trained to alert humans to the alarm, he'd heard that sound before and understood it meant trouble for his recipient. What motivated him to ignore his handler even though it would have been far easier for him simply to take the walk? How do we characterize Clyde and his relationship with Pam? Is he exclusively the genetic product of his wolf ancestors displaying concern for his alpha? Is he more like a young son who was afraid for his mother? Clyde is both the descendant of wolves and childlike in his devotion to Pam, but he is also much more. I think Pam explained

Clyde's role most accurately when she said, "He is my very best friend, and he was from the moment we met."

Best friend—that description works for me. But we must remember that our canine best friends aren't exactly like us. Those differences are part of what makes us such a formidable alliance. The more we understand about how dogs see and experience the world we share, the more worthy we become to share that friendship.

CHAPTER FOUR

Do You See What I See?

"Everything is okay now" was the first thing she said. In spite of her reassurance, I leapt to my feet and held out my hand so that Kent could give me the car keys. I knew Judy wouldn't have called unless something big—and probably bad—had happened.

At Canine Assistants, we have a long waiting list of people who need service dogs. Each applicant is evaluated based on the safety and suitability of the home for one of our dogs and how much a dog could realistically do to help the person physically, socially, and emotionally. Every other month, we hold a two-week "training camp," in which those who have finally reached the top of our waiting list come to Georgia to receive and learn how to work with a service dog of their own.

It was the second week of camp. The dogs, the recipients, and the staff were nervous and excited, an exhausting combination. In desperate need of a few hours off one evening, my husband and I left camp in the capable hands of Judy, our recipient coordinator, and went out to dinner with some friends. We had been seated only briefly when my cell phone rang. It was Judy. As I ran out of the restaurant, the phone pressed to my ear, she began to tell me the story.

Our students, both human and canine, were gathered in the lobby of the hotel in which they were staying before heading out for dinner. The dogs were all behaving admirably, with the exception of one usually mild-mannered golden retriever named Cottin. Cottin was growling at a young man in a long trench coat who was leaning against the registration desk, apparently waiting for someone. No matter who gave her the cue to be quiet, she would not stop making a low, throaty growl of warning. So primal and threatening was the sound, several of the people present said it gave them chills. Just as one of the group members was about to phone Cottin's trainer for help, six cars came squealing to a halt outside the hotel entrance. Federal agents jumped out, with guns drawn, and stormed the lobby, shouting, "Move, get down!"

Not particularly helpful instructions for a group of children who use wheelchairs; nevertheless, the agents quickly captured their man. But with all the confusion, it took everyone several moments to notice who that was: the man in the long trench coat, the one Cottin had been growling at—a man with an automatic weapon concealed beneath his coat and a record-breaking amount of cocaine in his hotel room. Moral of the story: Sometimes *dogs* know best.

How is it that dogs know what they know? Understanding how dogs collect and assess information about their environment requires a look at both their sense organs and their central processing center, the brain. The perceptual system of dogs, as is true for all species, has developed so that dogs may survive and flourish in their special niche in the world. Therefore, understanding how our dogs perceive things gives us insight into how they can best live and work with us.

Though a dog's brain is approximately 0.5 percent of the dog's total body mass, it utilizes more than 20 percent of the total oxygen intake. While structurally the brain of a dog and that of a human are similar, the dog's brain is approximately one-tenth the size. Some of the size difference can be attributed to the dog's modest cerebral cortex, the area of higher thinking, which is a much more substantial structure within the human brain. The human cerebral cortex consists of numerous folds that allow the brain to increase in surface area while reducing the amount of space needed to accommodate it. In larger mammals, the folds represent as much as two-thirds of the surface area of the cortex. A rat has a smooth cerebral cortex; a dog has a cerebral cortex with several folds; a human has a cerebral cortex with multiple folds.

Human cranial capacity has actually decreased by at least ten percent since the beginning of the Holocene period, approximately ten thousand years ago. While some of the reduction in size can be ascribed to the efficiency of the cerebral folds, archaeologist and anthropologist Dr. Colin Groves, from the Australian National University in Canberra, believes this reduction may also be the result of the strengthening of the relationship between man and dog. As man began to rely on the acute senses of his canine partner, he no longer needed to dedicate as much brain space to his own senses, ultimately leading to a decrease in mass.

Just how good are a dog's senses? During my early years at Canine Assistants, I learned a great deal about canine sensory perceptions, much of it, of course, from Nick.

It was around ten p.m., and I was, as usual for that time of night, in bed reading a book. I held the book in my left hand and scratched behind Nick's ears with my right. Nanny, who was spending a few nights with Mom and me, tapped lightly on my bedroom door. Nick looked up but didn't move. "Come in," I called. Nanny pushed the door open a little and poked her head into the room. In my grandmother's words, Nanny looked a sight. She had her hair up in rollers and her face completely slathered with a green face cream. As I started to tease her about her appearance, I realized that Nick had gone rigid and his mouth was pulled into a horrible snarl. He didn't recognize Nanny and was about to go after the weird-looking thing standing in our doorway. "It's Nanny, Nick," I said quickly. Nanny added her voice to mine, calling to Nick softly. As soon as he heard her familiar voice, Nick realized his mistake and lay back down, waiting for the petting to continue. Nanny slipped into the room, sat on the bed next to Nick, and took over the behind-the-ears scratching duty.

While Nanny's appearance had been somewhat altered, to me she was still easily identifiable as Nanny, but clearly she was not to Nick. I had always assumed that dogs had excellent vision. After all, weren't they supposed to be our sensory guides? In reality, dogs have rather limited vision. In order to understand the visual capabilities of dogs, we have to understand how the eye functions.

The retina of the eye contains two types of receptive nerve cells: cones and rods. Some cones are cells that help detect detail and rapid changes in images. This is visual acuity, the ability to see details clearly and individually. One indicator of visual acuity is the ratio of cones to retinal ganglion cells within the eye. Humans and other primates have the best visual acuity of all animals, with a ratio of 1:1. Studies have shown that dogs likely have a ratio of approximately 4:1, not nearly as good as that of humans. Functionally, this means that if you drew a one-by-two-inch rectangle and added twelve separate lines inside, a person could easily distinguish the individual lines, whereas a dog would see the shape as a solid blur.

To evaluate a person's visual acuity, ophthalmologists use what is known as the Snellen fraction. According to the Snellen fraction, the standard for human vision is 20/20. In contrast, a dog's vision is decidedly less sharp, something like 80/20. In other words, what we can see clearly from eighty feet away, dogs cannot see well until they are within twenty feet.

Other cone cells are responsible for color vision. I had always heard that dogs are color-blind. Not true; they simply have fewer cone photoreceptors than do humans. Most experts agree that dogs cannot see reds and greens but they can see yellows and blues. A red object would appear yellow to a dog, while a green object would be a grayish shade of white, similar to what people who are red–green color-blind see. There is also evidence that the colors dogs *do* see are not as vivid or saturated as the colors people see.

Though dogs are deficient in cones as compared to humans,

they have an abundance of rods, which are used for vision in low light. Some veterinary researchers claim that dogs see approximately five times better at night than humans do. Additionally, rods are used for motion detection. Dogs have the ability to see an object in motion from nearly twice as far away as they can see a stationary object, particularly in low light. Many dogs reflexively chase something when they see movement in their peripheral vision; they will leave stationary objects alone. This is a concept that Bob, my cat, has not yet been able to grasp. Bob, who is relentlessly chased by the dogs in my home, would be left alone if only he would remain still around them.

In addition to their profusion of rods, dogs have several other advantages that make them able to see in low light. The pupils of dogs' eyes can get much larger than those of humans, allowing dogs to take more of what light is available into their eyes. Dogs also have what's known as the *tapetum lucidum* in the back of their eyes, a surface that reflects light back through the retina for a second time. This *tapetum lucidum* is what causes dogs' eyes to often show up yellow in photographs.

Height also affects how and what dogs see. At Canine Assistants, we were having trouble getting our dogs to jump into the back of an SUV that had been donated to the program. They would willingly jump into the front or back seats, but the hatchback area seemed to be a "no-jump" zone. It took longer than I'd like to admit for me to understand what was causing their hesitation: From a dog's perspective, the black carpeting in the rear of the SUV looked like a bottomless pit. Light-colored towels spread across the back floor solved the problem instantly.

What dogs may lack in height and visual acuity, they more than make up for in auditory acuity. Hearing is measured in two ways: tone and volume. Dogs are able to hear a much wider range of tones than can humans. In order to reach the limit of a dog's hearing, we would have to add forty-eight new keys on the right (higher pitch) side of a piano keyboard, the last twenty of which would be imperceptible to humans. Dogs can even discern minimal changes and variations in tone. This sensitivity to sound can cause difficulties for dogs in human society, as they often hear things we cannot, such as the high-pitched sound emitted by the engine in a vacuum cleaner, painfully audible to dogs but undetectable to humans.

Meghan, my right hand at Canine Assistants, and I love the challenge of trying to fix the problems our dogs-in-training might be having. One day we took a service-dog-in-training on an outing to evaluate the young golden retriever's tendency, on rare occasions, to bark at seemingly nothing. We took the dog with us to lunch at a local restaurant, hoping it would turn into one of those rare occasions and we could analyze the dog's behavior together. As we walked to the restaurant, the dog's hackles went up, his ears perked up, he turned his head as if listening intently, and then he began to make a low growl at a nearby fire hydrant. The dog would alternately step toward the hydrant and then back away from it. He was absolutely terrified and was very clearly telling us so. The dog would not be comforted.

I looked at Meghan. "The dog definitely hears something," I said, stating the obvious. Yes, but what? Perhaps it was a whine caused by the internal flow of water beneath and through the hydrant, or a vibration emanating from its joints, or a hum coming from an electrical cable running beneath the sidewalk. In any case, we were not able to hear it ourselves, though we tried diligently. We will never know exactly what the dog was responding to, only that he heard something and was frightened by it. Over the course of time, we were able to desensitize him to odd sounds, but he always reacted when passing that particular hydrant.

In addition, dogs can hear sounds at a much lower volume than humans can. Remember the story of Clyde, the service dog who heard the respirator alarm of Pam, his recipient, while being walked outside? Clyde heard the sound from significantly farther away than Pam's daughter had.

When I was young, our family dog, Gigi, never got on the furniture (her choice) and wasn't much of a barker. It would have been completely out of character for her to bark incessantly or to act as an alarmist. But one Sunday morning, as she sat on my bed, she began to bark at the window that faced our neighbor's house. Promises of treats, toys, and even an early dinner did nothing to lure her away from the window. She would bark and whine at the neighbor's house, look back at us, and then repeat the cycle. Finally, my mother took her copy of the neighbor's house key, put Gigi on her leash, and the three of us walked next door. As soon as we reached the front door, Gigi began to scratch it frantically. We knew that Pauline, the neighbor, was home, so when our knocks went unanswered, we grew concerned and used the key to let ourselves in. As soon as the door opened, we could hear her calls for help. She had fallen thirty minutes earlier while getting out of the bathtub and broken her hip. Gigi had heard Pauline's cries from a bathroom on the opposite end of a 3,000-square-foot house, through who knows how many walls and across the side yard.

Dogs have such excellent hearing that we, as their caregivers, should be careful to avoid exposing them to stressful sounds. Loud, chaotic noises have been shown to increase stress in dogs. Whenever Mom and I would take Nick in the car with us, Mom would ask me to turn the radio volume down. "Nick doesn't like it loud," she'd say. Turns out experts agree with her; Nick probably didn't like loud music.

The ability to discern touch is developed very early in a puppy's life. Puppies are born with receptors in their faces so they can feel for their mother should they become separated before their eyes have opened. And touch remains important to the health and well-being of dogs throughout their lives.

Dogs perceive, as do humans, four forms of touch: pressure, heat, and cold, pain, and proprioception (the ability to tell where one's limbs are and how rapidly parts of the body are moving). The most sensitive areas for touch on a dog are the muzzle, nose, and the paws, particularly between the toes. The receptors in the paws are thought to help dogs sense vibration and determine the stability of surfaces on which they are walking. The whiskers on a dog are also considered by researchers to be of great importance, helping a dog orient himself to his environment and functioning much like the cane of a person who is visually impaired.

Many people use tight T-shirts or body wraps to soothe anxious dogs, much like the way we swaddle newborns. Some behaviorists believe that this constant touch of the cloth simulates being in the womb and makes dogs feel safe. Others attribute the effectiveness of the wrap to helping the dog feel more in touch with his physical body.

My sister-in-law had a day when she wished she didn't feel so in touch with her physical body. She became acutely ill the morning after eating a fish dinner from a chain-type seafood restaurant. To this day, some twenty years later, the very sight of the restaurant's logo brings to mind the experience and makes her queasy. I have known other people who've had similar experiences and responses. Dogs, too, have the capability to remember a taste that they associate with making them sick in the past.

Too many treats from my mom led Nick to gain an unacceptable amount of weight. In an effort to reverse that trend, I put him on a diet, part of which included no-salt green beans as a snack. One day, after I applied a new topical flea treatment to his back, I gave Nick an extra-large helping of green beans. Several hours later, Nick began to vomit profusely. Though the cause was most likely the flea medication rather than the green beans, Nick was convinced the vegetable was at fault. For the rest of his life, Nick turned up his nose when he saw green beans. It seems both humans and dogs have the same defense mechanism against repeatedly eating harmful substances.

However, horse manure clearly seems not to be considered a toxic substance by most dogs. My dogs look at it as a delicious treat, something like oatmeal cookies. Eating substances that humans find repulsive is very much a dog thing. Many dogs even help keep the yard clean by eating the poop of other dogs.

Perhaps dogs can tolerate things that would sicken us because they do not have much ability to taste. While people boast an impressive average of 9,000 taste buds, dogs can claim only a paltry 1,706. Even so, they do seem to have the ability to perceive the big-five tastes: sweet, salty, bitter, sour, and savory.

Experts agree that most dogs tend to favor sweet tastes and do not like bitter ones, while seeming to have ambivalence for salty ones. Experts also agree that dogs, like humans, have a strong preference for foods associated with positive emotional experiences. If this is true, then my dogs must all have extremely fond memories involving Milk-Bone's soft and chewy treats.

Taste, for dogs and people, is strongly influenced by smell. Smell leads us to the most phenomenal of all sensory input tools: the nose of a dog. A fable based on biblical lore is said to explain why a dog's nose is wet. As the story goes, the two dogs on Noah's Ark were responsible for patrolling the boat to check on the well-being of the other animals. One day, while on their rounds, the dogs discovered a small leak in the boat's hull. Realizing that a leak meant grave trouble, one dog ran for help while the other used his long nose to plug the hole until help arrived. God was so pleased that he commanded that henceforth all dogs would have cold, wet noses to commemorate their intelligence and bravery.

Though I cannot attest to the authenticity of that story, I do know that dogs are capable of doing remarkable things with their noses. Proportionally, the brain of a dog devotes forty times more space to smell than does that of a human. Rather than being sorted through the part of the brain that handles the other four senses, input from the nose is sent directly to a special area of the dog's brain, the paleocortex, which begins instantly to decipher the data. In addition to the standard scent receptors in their noses, dogs have a vomeronasal organ that opens into the nose and has its own set of receptors, increasing exponentially the amount of scent detail collected. The nose of a dog is so sensitive that it is difficult for even scientists to quantify. Estimates of their scent-discrimination abilities range from 1,000 to 100,000 times that of humans. In addition, dogs can smell each component of an odor. The best explanation of this ability I've heard is that rather than smelling beef stew, dogs smell meat, celery, onion, potato, carrot, and each component of the sauce.

Lynn, a friend of our family, has a golden retriever, Molson, whom she now refers to as "the best breast man in all fifty states." Several years ago, Molson began sniffing and pawing at Lynn's left breast. He was absolutely relentless in his inspection. Occasionally, he would growl and whine after sniffing her. Finally, Lynn was so distressed by his behavior that she made an appointment with her doctor. She was subsequently diagnosed with a small malignant mass in her left breast. Thanks to Molson's early detection, Lynn is now cancer-free and has a great prognosis for a healthy future. Of course, I wouldn't suggest leaving your health care to your dog; not all dogs have noses as sensitive as Molson's.

Prison officials are using dogs to sniff out contraband cell phones. Customs agents use dogs trained to detect drugs and other contraband. A beagle brigade is dedicated to detecting illegally imported fruits and vegetables that might be harmful to agriculture. Dogs are used to sniff out skin cancer, low blood sugar, mold, and even peanuts for those who have peanut allergies. An eight-year-old Colorado girl, Riley, has a peanut-detection dog name Rock'O. Riley's peanut allergy is so severe that she once accidentally caught a piece of peanut shell in her sandal and nearly had to have a skin graft. Riley used to have to wear gloves to school to avoid accidentally touching peanut residue. Now Rock'O, a big Portuguese water dog, goes everywhere with Riley and sits in his "alert" posture when he smells something dangerous.

A bloodhound, often referred to as "a nose with a dog attached," is said to have approximately 230 million olfactory cells. In 1993, a bloodhound named Yogi found the body of a missing five-year-old girl, Alie, under remarkable circumstances. A canine officer with the Aurora, Colorado, police department, Yogi was called in to search for the child three days after her disappearance. Authorities believed that Yogi was unlikely to succeed in his efforts because the kidnapper had most likely driven the girl away, and several hundred people had already trampled the crime scene in the search effort. Yogi was not deterred, however. He began his search at the steps of Alie's apartment complex, having been given a piece of her clothing to smell. Yogi immediately found the trail. He sniffed down one of the busiest streets in the Denver area and straight to the interstate highway. Officers drove Yogi to each exit until the dog identified the exit taken by the kidnapper. After reaching Deer Creek Canyon and working some seven hours in blazing heat, Yogi's trainer suspended the search for the night. The officer handling the dog said he knew Yogi would have continued his efforts until he dropped from exhaustion.

The following morning, officers began to comb the area around the canyon and found Alie's body about a mile from where Yogi had stopped his search the previous night. In all, Yogi had followed the three-day-old scent of the child, who was being driven in a car, for ten miles down busy streets and even on the expressway. In his seven-year career, Yogi worked 476 cases in eight states, helping to convict twenty-seven murderers. He found robbers, escaped prisoners, Alzheimer's patients who had wandered away from home, drunk drivers who had left the scene of accidents, and even people trapped in collapsed buildings. Just a few days before Yogi died of cancer in 1998, he was involved in a manhunt for the killer of a Denver police officer.

In my work at Canine Assistants, I am constantly reminded of how important it is that people who live with dogs be able to, metaphorically speaking, see the world through a dog's eyes. If we don't at least try to understand how our dogs perceive our shared environment, we end up being unfair to our dogs and ourselves. One of our recipients, Stan, nearly lost his life, as well as the trust of his dog, Longly, one day because he did not understand that his dog had vital sensory information he was desperately trying to share. Stan was sound asleep one night when Longly began to paw him repeatedly. Stan sheepishly admits that, when telling his dog to get off the bed didn't work, he lost his temper and shouted at him. Longly's tail instantly tucked in fear and contrition, but he still didn't get off the bed.

Finally, as Longly dragged Stan by his pajama pants toward his wheelchair parked beside the bed, Stan smelled the scent his dog had recognized far earlier—smoke. The house was on fire. Had his dog not alerted him to the smoke, Stan might well have remained asleep until it was too late to escape. These days, we spend a great deal of time during our training camps encouraging our recipients to understand and respect their dogs' sensory abilities and limitations.

CHAPTER FIVE

The Canine Mystique

Nick loved me dearly, of that I am certain, but he had special insight when it came to my mom. Mom had horrible osteoporosis. More months than not, she had at least one fracture in her back, ribs, or foot. The muscle spasms that she had in conjunction with the fractures were terribly painful. Mom hid the hurt particularly well. Often, I couldn't tell when the spasms had begun, but Nick always knew. As soon as the spasms started, he would commence barking at her and would not stop until Mom finally gave up and excused herself to go lie down. Then he would be quiet.

Every year, Mom traveled to Florida to visit her brother and sister-in-law. On the morning of her scheduled return, Nick would wake early, pawing restlessly at me with excited energy. Mom always took the same flight home, arriving in Atlanta just after noon. By ten a.m. on those mornings, Nick would have grabbed my purse at least five times, ready to head to the airport to pick her up. Each time she went, Nick knew when she was coming home. How was that possible? I assumed he was reading some subtle cue from me that I didn't realize I was giving. I was wrong.

One early morning, the day before Mom was scheduled to arrive, Nick woke me. I tried in every way possible to explain that she wasn't coming back until the following day. Nick would have none of it. He continued to get my purse and sit at the back door, waiting to jump into the car, ready to head to the airport. I was starting to think he was going to sit there the entire day when the phone rang.

"Don't leave for the airport yet. My flight is an hour late," Mom said.

"But, Mom, you aren't coming back until the third. That's tomorrow," I answered.

Mom laughed. "Honey, today is the third, and I am about to get on the plane home." She paused for a moment. "Didn't Nick tell you?" Yes, he told me. I just didn't listen.

Extrasensory perception (ESP) can be defined as perception not explainable using the prescribed abilities of the five traditional senses. The potential for ESP in dogs is a subject that has fascinated their owners for years. Indeed, those of us who love dogs would like nothing better than to prove to the rest of the world what we already know—that dogs have wondrous, mystical powers.

Dr. Rupert Sheldrake, biochemist and author of *Dogs That Know When Their Owners Are Coming Home: And Other Unexplained Powers of Animals,* believes that dogs—indeed, many animals—have extrasensory perception. Dr. Sheldrake has spent much of his career investigating three major categories of ESP in animals: telepathy, homing, and premonitions.

Telepathy is the ability to convey information in a way that cannot be attributed to the five known senses. Dr. Sheldrake's belief in telepathy is based on his views concerning the critical nature of social bonds, meaning that, by definition, all members of a group share some fundamental bond. There are intraspecies bonds, such as those between a mother wolf and her pups, and there are interspecies bonds, like those between a dog and his human caregiver.

Dr. Sheldrake believes that these bonds exist within what he terms morphic fields, fields that "hold together and coordinate the parts of a system in space and time, and contain a memory from previous similar systems."

Sheldrake likes to use elastic bands to explain his theories. Imagine a family held together by a big super-stretchy rubber band. If one member of the family is moved away from the others, no matter how far, the rubber band stretches to continue accommodating them all. Now add bungee cords directly connecting each family member. While most people view the connection between individuals as metaphorical, Dr. Sheldrake believes that they are not metaphorical in the least but are very much literal. In other words, our "bungee cords" exist in the physical world—we just can't see them. It's almost like a wireless phone connection, allowing for communication between the members of a group regardless of how far away they may be from one another.

In his younger days, my husband, Kent, went diving in the Florida Keys with his college marine-biology class. While his friend Dan was ninety feet down, his regulator valve malfunctioned, rapidly emptying his tank of air. The water was unusually murky, and Dan wasn't able to signal Kent that he was in trouble; he had to swim to find him, losing precious moments. By the time Dan reached Kent, his air was gone. At a depth of ninety feet, you can't just bolt up without risking decompression sickness. You have to ascend thirty feet at a time and then pause to let your body acclimate to the change in pressure. Though Kent's air supply was dangerously low, the pair headed up as quickly as they dared, buddy-breathing what air remained. By the time they left their final acclimation point at thirty feet under the surface, their air was completely gone. Though they made it to the surface, they were shaken to their cores.

Meanwhile, nearly 2,000 miles away, Kent's mother was overcome by the feeling that her oldest son was in trouble. She had no idea where he was or what he was doing, she knew only that something wasn't right. So acute were her feelings of distress that she contacted the members of her church and asked that they pray for Kent's safety. Relief swept through her when Kent called home, told her the story, and, more important, confirmed that he was fine.

My dear friend Carolyn and I don't have the opportunity to

speak on a regular basis, but we share a very strong bond. Many times in the past, I began to think about calling Carolyn but, before I could, she would phone me. So regular are these episodes that I almost feel I have the ability to summon her calls. And my curious connections to those I love do not seem limited to people.

One day, Rowland, a close friend, and I were on our way out to dinner and drove by the barn where I stabled my horses. We had seen the horses several hours earlier and all was well. Yet, as we reached the driveway, I cried, "Turn in! The horses are loose." Rowland was so badly startled by my shouting that he turned without braking, squealing into the complex. As we crested the hill, there were my horses, munching grass outside their stalls. My heart was pounding with the knowledge that they could have easily run out the main gate and into the busy road. It wasn't until after we had gotten the horses safely back into their stalls and reinforced the latches on their doors that Rowland asked me how I had known the horses were loose. There was no way I could have seen them from the road, and they had never gotten out before, so I couldn't have been responding to a known potential. My response to Rowland: *"I just knew."*

Under Dr. Sheldrake's model, we could say that my morphic connection with the horses allowed me to "tune" in to their current state. Can our dogs do that with us? Can they telepathically tune in to our state even when many miles separate us?

In 1927, J. B. Rhine, who later became known as the father of parapsychology, joined Duke University's faculty to pursue research into ESP and psychic phenomena. During his time there, Rhine and his wife, Louisa, conducted a number of experiments related to the potential paranormal abilities of animals. In his book *Extra-Sensory Perception,* published in 1934, Rhine stated: "The number of re- ported cases on animal ESP is large enough to suggest that animals can somehow be affected by circumstances they could not be aware of by any sensory sign and which one would suppose they could hardly understand in human terms."

In more-modern times, Dr. Sheldrake has gathered numerous anecdotal reports of potential psychic ability in animals, particularly evidence of telepathic capability. This behavior has been most easily observed in the cases of animals who are seemingly able to sense the return home of their owners.

One of the most incredible of the numerous owner stories related to Dr. Sheldrake involved a Labrador retriever who lived on base with his owner, an officer in the Royal Air Force. When the officer was out on a mission, the dog would rest quietly. When his plane was approaching, the dog would leap to his feet excitedly. Even though other planes could be heard, the dog jumped up only for his owner's incoming aircraft. Squadron members assumed that the dog recognized the particular sound of the engines on the officer's aircraft, until the day the dog failed to get up for the plane. Those watching assumed it was a rare instance of the dog missing the approach, but when the plane landed, his owner was not on it. Later, the Lab jumped up and frantically wagged his tail when a different aircraft approached from a different direction. Sure enough, the dog's owner was on that plane.

As a scientist, Dr. Sheldrake knew that anecdotal reports alone could not be used to prove that the phenomenon existed, so he set up controlled experiments in an effort to verify the evidence. His first experiment centered on a woman named Pam and her terrier mix, Jaytee.

Pam had adopted Jaytee from a shelter when he was a puppy. For several years, Pam's family had been telling her that they knew when she was coming home, because Jaytee would always go to the window to watch for her arrival. Pam's parents were particularly impressed because Jaytee continued to predict Pam's return even after she lost her job, from which her arrival times were fairly regular, and began to go out for irregular periods. When Pam read that Dr. Sheldrake was looking for subjects with whom to conduct his research, Pam volunteered Jaytee and herself.

First, Dr. Sheldrake had Pam and her parents keep a log detailing when she went out, her method of transportation, what time she started home, and what time she arrived. In total, information was recorded for one hundred trials. In eighty-five out of the hundred times, Jaytee went to the window ten minutes or more prior to

Pam's arrival home. When the log was further analyzed, they realized that Jaytee went to the window just as Pam was starting for home, regardless of how far away she was, a significant number of times. And of the fifteen times that Jaytee did not alert Pam's parents to her return, only three couldn't be easily explained by distractions such as Jaytee being ill or a neighbor's dog being in season. Dr. Sheldrake decided this pair merited further investigation.

In order to eliminate any possibility that Jaytee was recognizing the sound of Pam's car, she was asked to travel by other means such as taxi, bicycle, or train. Jaytee continued to anticipate her return. To negate the chance that Jaytee was responding to some subconscious cue from Pam's parents, the parents were not told of her schedule. Jaytee still knew. To rule out the possibility that Jaytee was simply going to the window more often the longer Pam was gone, her absence times were varied. Jaytee went to the window the most and stayed the longest when Pam was headed home. Finally, in order to eliminate any chance that "wishful thinking" was interfering with accurate reporting of the data by Pam's family, Dr. Sheldrake decided to videotape Jaytee while Pam was away.

From May 1995 to June 1996, a camera was set up for thirty trials in Pam's parents' house in front of the window from which Jaytee was said to watch for Pam's return. In these trials, Pam was allowed to determine her own return time but wasn't allowed to share that time with her parents. She was also asked to vary the length of her absences. Jaytee spent around 10 percent of his time at the window when Pam was away. That percentage jumped to more than 30 when Pam was thinking about her return and went to almost 60 percent when Pam was on her way home. The results were statistically significant, though of course there were skeptics and detractors.

In my experience with dogs and their owners, I have become convinced that some people have a deeper connection with animals than do others. At Canine Assistants, we have had several recipients or their family members claim to be able to communicate telepathically with dogs. During one training camp, the husband of a recipient felt that his ability to understand our dogs was so clear and precise that he began to report to the other recipients exactly what he heard their dogs saying. For the most part, his translations were upbeat statements like "I love my new mom" or "I enjoy working." Trouble came, however, when the man translated the supposed musings of Benjamin, a young golden, who had been placed with a precious eight-year-old girl named Sara Beth. According to this man, Benjamin used foul and unrepeatable language almost exclusively. Sara Beth was horrified and tearfully told me she wouldn't be able to take her dog out in public since all he said were naughty words. After a brief talk with me, the purported psychic explained to Sara Beth that he had misinterpreted her dog because Benjamin spoke only Spanish, a language he himself did not speak.

Not all of our self-proclaimed pet psychics were nutty. Several people seemed genuinely able to communicate with our dogs in unique ways. One woman could call dogs to her by "using her mind to tap into theirs." I watched this woman repeatedly coax dogs across our training-room floor and into her lap, and I could never see a trick. She didn't seem to move or vocalize at all.

In addition to telepathy, dogs have been credited with a homing instinct that allows them to find their way home over great distances. There are reportedly two different types of homing instinct: One refers to a dog's ability to follow his owner when the owner has moved to a new location; the other refers to a dog's ability to return to its own home after being away. Dramatic stories of dogs demonstrating both types of homing instinct abound.

Though many of the stories about dogs finding their way home are undoubtedly true, they create for scientists an interesting dilemma. Repeated experiments have shown that dogs cannot find their way home on their own from long distances using their five senses alone. If dogs do have a homing instinct, its source is a mystery. But then, dogs seem to have all sorts of mysterious powers, such as the ability to respond to the death of their owners even from a distance and to sense when their owners are in peril.

Some animals even show signs of precognition—the ability to anticipate future events. Such is the story of a cat who lived in a nursing home and seemed to know when a patient was close to death. He would sit in the patient's room, a sort of feline grim reaper. Over time the cat successfully anticipated the death of twenty-five patients.

During World War II, many families used their dogs to alert them to oncoming air raids. In London, the Evans family claimed their Lab, Buddy, was the early-warning system for their entire neighborhood. When Buddy would whine and scratch on the front door, Mr. Evans would go into the yard and blow his bugle to let the neighbors know they should head for the air-raid shelter. Buddy never failed to sound the alert long before the air-raid sirens, and he never missed a raid. Lest we attribute his uncanny ability to a highly developed sense of hearing, Buddy was born without the ability to hear.

How Buddy knew the planes were coming remains a mystery. Also mysterious is the ability of many dogs to anticipate earthquakes or other natural disasters. Some researchers claim that the animals can feel vibrations from the ground that alert them to something unusual.

At Canine Assistants, there are dogs who know when their human partners are going to have a seizure. Some can give warning as far in advance as an hour, though most alerts come between ten and forty minutes prior to the onset. Whether or not dogs truly can anticipate seizures is a question that has merited study and debate. Neurologists and scientists wondered if the anecdotal reports were clouded, once again, by "wishful thinking."

I have seen this phenomenon play out hundreds of times and can state without hesitation that some dogs have this ability, though I do not know in advance which dogs will demonstrate it. My experience has led me to believe that most, if not all, dogs probably possess the ability to recognize certain oncoming seizures. Whether or not an individual dog provides an early warning or the person recognizes the warning signal is based in large part on the depth of the bond between person and dog. All of our dogs are taught the necessary skills to work with people who have seizure disorders and mobility problems. This way, we are able to base placement exclusively on how well the pair bonds.

I cannot tell you how the dogs know or to what they are responding. If we could determine that, training would be quicker, more effective, and considerably easier, allowing more dogs to be placed with those who would benefit greatly by such early warning. Imagine what this could mean to someone with epilepsy—no more being afraid to leave the house for fear of having a seizure in public; no more falling, splitting open foreheads, and knocking teeth loose; no more living with constant dread. The relief almost defies imagination. Yet, after working with dogs for many years, I find myself only slightly closer to the answer of how than I was the first time I considered the possibilities.

I have come to believe that there are several ways in which dogs might recognize an approaching seizure. My initial theory was that dogs could be sensing an electrical change in the person's body, a short-circuiting in the brain that had not yet had a discernible effect on the person. However, after watching a tape of one of our recipients in an epilepsy-monitoring unit, I changed my mind.

In an effort to better understand his particular case of epilepsy, doctors hooked the young man, Taylor, up to an EEG machine, which continuously monitored the electrical activity in his brain. As is routine in such monitoring, cameras were also set up to film any activity in the room. Chelsea, a large golden retriever, had been with Taylor for only six weeks, but the two had formed an intense bond. As with most of the matches made at Canine Assistants, Chelsea seemed to pick Taylor as her recipient. The connection was clear from the first time they were paired together. Chelsea was with Taylor in the monitoring unit, and the videotape shows her clearly alerting in advance of both the seizures he had while there. When comparing the tape to the EEG tracings, there was absolutely no electrical change in Taylor's brain until he actively started to seize, several minutes after Chelsea began her alert.

I then thought that perhaps dogs were so attuned to their owners that they could detect even slightly odd behavior. However, I reasoned, it was hard to believe that a dog would notice behavioral changes that even a mother, actively looking for those changes, could not. Furthermore, seizure dogs often do not need to be in the same room as their owner to sense a seizure and alert someone to it. We have had many dogs jump up from naps in other rooms to signal an oncoming event.

The most commonly cited theory of how dogs are able to predict seizures is based on smell. It is thought that the dog recognizes a unique, particular odor emitted by the person prior to onset. Dogs' noses are infinitely more powerful than humans can comprehend, but are we to assume that dogs smell an oncoming seizure simply because we know they can smell well? While the effects of a seizure play out in various parts of the body, the process happens entirely within the brain. If we cannot see any changes in the brain prior to the onset of the seizure, what could possibly be producing an odor?

In the end, seizure prediction is but one more addition to the list of abilities possessed by dogs and not understood by man. That dogs have *extraordinary* sensory perception is undeniable, and we will surely continue to discover new ways in which they use these remarkable abilities. But are these abilities *extrasensory*? The answer to that question is yet to be determined, but, regardless of which sensory perception is at work, my life with Nick and the dogs of Canine Assistants has taught me that they are magical, wondrous creatures that possess amazing gifts. Would it somehow lessen those gifts if future research proved that one of the traditional five senses is what makes these abilities possible? Of course it would not; just ask one of the recipients of our seizure response dogs. Dogs have abilities of the mind and senses that go way beyond what I ever thought possible. Since we are far from discovering all that they are capable of, we should remain open to the potential of their mystique.

CHAPTER SIX

Canine Cognition

I first realized how smart Nick was when our two-person, one-dog (at the time) household began to consume massive amounts of peanut butter crackers. Mom thought it was me; I thought it was her. Perplexed by how my tiny mother was consuming four to five packages, eight crackers to the pack, a day, I finally asked her about it. She denied it. I knew it wasn't me. That left only one possibility: Nick. When no one was paying attention, Nick would slip into the kitchen and tug open the drawer with the crackers in it, take out a single pack, nose the drawer closed, and take the crackers behind the living-room couch to eat in peace. He never took the whole box and always closed the drawer. He went into the room we were the least likely to enter. Those weren't actions indicating that he "knew he was being naughty" or "felt guilty." Rather, he understood that if we saw him we would move the crackers out of his reach—a brilliant deduction by an incredibly brilliant dog.

Dogs are clearly capable of taking information into their brains. But what do they do with the information? How exactly do they think? Consider for a moment that you are trying to decide on a restaurant. Isn't your internal reasoning carried out primarily in words? Indeed, most of us do think in words. But what happens if you don't have an extensive vocabulary? Or *any,* for that matter?

Some scientists contend that deliberative thought cannot occur without words. However, noted animal researcher Temple Grandin disputes this concept in her book *Animals in Translation.* Grandin suggests that animals and people like herself, who have autism, think in pictures rather than words. This theory makes a great deal more sense than accepting the notion that dogs cannot think simply because they lack words.

Studies on how a creature thinks or what it knows are notoriously difficult to conduct when the animal does not share our language, and for most of the twentieth century, little research was done on animal cognition. However, animals were being used in laboratory experiments. In the 1920s, Ivan Pavlov was researching salivation in dogs when he observed that many of the dogs began to salivate before the food was within range of sight or smell, indicating that they were picking up on a cue other than the food itself. This denoted a higher brain function than mere reflexive salivation. Yet Pavlov was not edging toward the concept that animals have higher intelligence; he believed his experiment allowed for the examination of dogs' nervous systems "without any need to resort to fantastic speculations as to the existence of any possible subjective state in the animal which may be conjectured on analogy with ourselves." In other words, he wasn't buying humanlike intelligence in the animals.

Pavlov's theories in classical conditioning gave rise to the science known as behaviorism. Classical behaviorism regards all the things that organisms do—including thinking and feeling—as behaviors. B. F. Skinner, an American psychologist, developed his own school of thought, called radical behaviorism, in the middle of the last century. Radical behaviorism seeks to understand behavior as a function of previous environmental experiences and reinforcing consequences. In dog terms: *Last time I sat when she said "sit," I got a cookie, so I think I'll sit again when she asks.* Skinner's ideas led to operant conditioning—the idea that positive and negative reinforcements and punishments could be used to shape behavior.

Skinner never ascribed thoughts or feelings to animals; rather, he considered an individual animal a "black box" that stored all functions of mind and body resulting in behavior. Skinner believed that there was no need to understand what was happening inside the black box in order to predict behavior. Many of today's popular trainers and behaviorists still take Skinner's approach when working with dogs, noting only the stimulus that produces a behavior, not how the dog processes the stimulus. For example, if a dog jumps on people when they come into the house, Skinnerians would seek only to change the dog's behavior, rather than trying first to comprehend what has caused the behavior and then effecting change based on that understanding.

The field of ethology, the study of animal behavior in the animal's natural environment, dates back to the 1930s, though it wasn't until the 1980s that the number of researchers focusing on dogs increased dramatically. Some researchers believe that we are in a "golden age" of ethology-oriented research, and thanks to ethologists, we now understand a great deal about animal behavior outside the laboratory.

Advances in science and investigative methods aside, some in the scientific community still believe no animal is capable of rational thought. They contend that animals merely react to stimuli without contemplation, much like a machine, albeit a somewhat complex machine. I would ask you to explain away the abilities of animals such as Washoe, a chimp who was taught American Sign Language by a young graduate assistant named Roger Fouts at the Institute of Primate Studies in Oklahoma in the late 1960s.

By the age of five, Washoe was using 132 signs correctly and could understand hundreds of other signs. Washoe even started to combine words she knew into phrases that made sense—an ability known as syntax, long held to be the hallmark of human communication.

In the fall of 1999, a friend sent me a copy of an article in *The New York Times* about an African gray parrot named Alex. What I learned about Alex from that article and further reading had a profound effect on the way I thought about animals. In the late 1970s, a scientist named Irene Pepperberg wanted to study language acquisition and cognition potential in a nonprimate. Alex was her first subject. Under Dr. Pepperberg's creative tutelage, Alex learned to speak, label objects with words, and even create words of his own such as "banerry," which he used to signify an apple—most probably a combination of the taste of a banana and the color of a cherry. Creating a new word by putting two words together is called lexical elision, and it is indicative of notable cognitive processes such as labeling, word comprehension, and categorization. Alex could count and proved himself capable of understanding what numbers—including zero—signified. He could recognize like and different objects and group them accordingly. Alex was vocal about his distress when he was separated from Dr. Pepperberg. He told her that he loved her and acted accordingly. Alex was clever, manipulative, creative, and highly emotional.

For the first time, a nonhuman animal was verbalizing thoughts and feelings. If Alex, a bird, had intelligent thoughts and deep feelings, so, too, must other animals. It occurred to me then that the only difference between Alex and a dog was the ability to speak in a way we could understand.

Alex's voice opened the door for studies on other nonprimates and, finally, the scientific community turned its attention to dogs. Animal psychologist Juliane Kaminski studied Rico, a border collie, in Germany and published the results of her findings in *Science* magazine in June 2004. Rico demonstrated an ability to pick out a new object from a number of familiar ones even when asked to do so with an unfamiliar word. To reason by exclusion is called fast mapping—the ability to match a new word with a previously unknown entity by excluding known entities.

Dr. Kaminski and her colleagues also realized that dogs, when told to "leave" a treat placed in front of them, would leave the treat if the researcher's eyes were open but would take it if the researcher's eyes were closed. This is an important piece of information about the intelligence of dogs, because it shows the capability to understand the situation of another. This research is borne out every day at Canine Assistants, as I watch dogs come to recognize the circumstances of their recipients and adjust their behavior to fit the need.

A study was recently conducted by Dr. Friederike Range and colleagues at the University of Vienna in Austria in which two dogs were asked to put a paw in a researcher's hand, but only one dog was rewarded for so doing. The dog who wasn't rewarded eventually stopped participating, suggesting that he recognized the unfairness of not receiving a treat. Anyone who has multiple dogs could have told researchers that dogs indeed are concerned with fairness. I always count out the same number of treats for each of my four dogs or risk being pestered relentlessly by the dog I shorted. In fact, my goldendoodle Jack will not eat or chew a bone if his three buddies are not also fed approximately the same thing. That my dogs demand an equal number of treats is evidence of the quantitative assessment skills of dogs. In my experience, dogs can, to some extent, count.

Notwithstanding the story on fairness, Jack isn't always about equality. When my other goldendoodle Butch has a toy that Jack wants, Jack runs to the front door and barks as if someone is about to knock. Butch immediately drops the toy and runs to the door to aid in raising the alarm. Then Jack slips back and nabs the toy.

But poor Butch doesn't always get the short end of the stick. When he was only eighteen months old, he occasionally liked to chew on my son's toys, even after many hours spent patiently teaching him they were off-limits. As soon as Butch captured his booty, he would run into our den, jump up on the couch, and begin to chew. Hiding behind a door, I was able to observe his behavior on several occasions. When Butch heard a person coming toward the den, he would pull the blanket off the back of the couch to cover his stolen item; he removed it only when he believed he was alone. This skit indicated that Butch was capable of deception, by hiding the toy; self-recognition and empathy, in knowing that we, separate and distinct entities from him, would take the toy if we saw it; and intention, by taking his booty only to the couch that had a blanket hanging on the back. Butch was not indicating he understood that he would get in trouble for having the toy (that is, "knowing better") but simply and instinctively did not want the toy taken away—behavior reminiscent of Nick and his peanut butter crackers.

Having watched Nick push a footstool over so he could climb up to reach a toy on a high shelf, I have long believed some dogs understand the notion of "means to an end." To further test that theory, I decided to re-create an experiment I'd read about. I tied a string around a large Milk-Bone and, after showing the treat to several dogs, put it through a small hole in a wooden fence. In order to get the biscuit, the dogs had to pull it back through the fence hole by using the string. All five of the young adult dogs I tested figured out how to manipulate the string to reach the treat within three minutes. Consider this for a moment: Not only does this ability show a grasp of "means to an end," it is similar to that skill long thought to be the province only of primates—tool usage.

Cooperation requires understanding the concept of self and other. Dogs can cooperate brilliantly with one another and with humans. They herd with us, hunt with us, and patrol with us. Consider dogs who guide those who have impaired vision; moving safely from place to place is a collaborative effort of the highest order.

I have a friend who was totally stumped by the fact that apples kept disappearing from her kitchen counter. Though she had one dog who was clearly tall enough to reach the countertop, she had tried on multiple occasions to feed the dog apples, without success. On the other hand, the woman's smaller dog loved apples but wasn't tall enough to reach the counter. Sure enough, it turned out the bigger dog was knocking the apples off the counter for her smaller cohort.

At Canine Assistants, we often use a concept known as overnight learning to teach our dogs difficult behaviors, such as flicking on a switch with their nose. Much as in humans, new ideas or knowledge jells in dogs' brains overnight. We know that dogs dream much like humans, so perhaps this is when the jelling takes place. Many times have I put up a dog one evening believing that he had not yet grasped a new concept, only to have the dog run out first thing the following morning and execute it perfectly.

Butch did this to me one night when I was trying to teach him to carry a bag. Butch would retrieve the bag and give it to me, but he didn't seem to grasp the idea of carrying the bag himself. After the training session, I went to bed feeling as if I had failed in my efforts.

At about five o'clock the next morning, Butch woke me with great exuberance, asking to start the day. I, not so patiently, explained that he would have to wait because it was too early to get up. After a few restless minutes, I could no longer stand the sound of Butch pacing back and forth beside the bed, so I cracked open one eye, prepared to fuss again. What did I see? Butch walking up and down proudly, holding the bag I'd tried to teach him to carry the previous night. This is an excellent example to show that dogs can retain and manipulate abstract images. Another word for this process: thought.

Recently, one of my heroes in the dog world, Dr. Adam Miklosi, the director of the Family Dog Project at Eötvös Loránd University in Budapest, came to visit us at Canine Assistants. I love listening to him talk about the project's work with dogs, especially their cognition studies. He is a gifted man, and I am convinced that all dogs will benefit significantly from the work Adam and his colleagues are doing. That is certainly what Adam hopes, as he believes that the role of their research is largely to provide useful information to those of us who live and work with dogs.

Two of the recent studies conducted at the Family Dog Project intrigued me so much that I decided to replicate modified versions of them at Canine Assistants. My first effort sought to evaluate the contention that dogs can convey information to their human partners in order to accomplish a common goal. If the dogs realized that their owners lacked vital information, would they attempt to provide it?

I asked three Canine Assistants trainers to participate, using dogs with whom they shared a strong attachment. The trainers each chose a toy their dog really enjoyed playing with. I then asked the trainers to label that toy with a name. Hetty, a Lab, loved a fuzzy, squeaky toy in the shape of a person, so her trainer labeled it "Woolly Man." As soon as Hetty showed that she understood the question "Where's Woolly Man?" the trainer left the room and Hetty watched as I hid the toy in a closet. When the trainer returned, I had her ask Hetty, "Where's Woolly Man?" In the first trial, it took the dog twenty-one seconds to run to the closet and paw at the door. The process was repeated nine additional times, and during each, the toy was hidden in a new place known to the dog but not the trainer. The length of time it took Hetty to point out the hidden location decreased with each trial. By the eighth trial, she ran immediately to the hiding place upon the trainer's return. Similar results were seen with the other two trainer–dog teams, offering strong evidence that dogs can and will provide information to their human partners in order to reach a common goal.

The purpose of the next experiment I re-created was to provide evidence that dogs can replicate behaviors shown them by people. During his visit, Adam played a video demonstrating one dog's ability to "do as I do" with his owner. I watched in amazement as a man bowed toward his dog, only to have the dog bow in return. Next, the man took a cup and placed it in a nearby trash can. He then asked his dog to "do it," and the dog immediately picked up a similar cup and dropped it into the can. Over and over, the dog copied his owner's actions, often having to substitute his mouth for his owner's hand in order to accomplish the task.

I began by teaching my dog Jack to "do as I do" with behaviors that he already knew on cue, such as "down." That way I could lie on the floor, ask Jack to "do it," and then give him the cue to "down." I needed to do that only once. Instantly, Jack learned to "do it" without needing any other cue. He was a natural. Now I've taught him to open a cabinet, remove a loaf of bread, and place it on a nearby table by copying my actions. From a cognitive standpoint, this ability indicates, among other things, that dogs can retain and manipulate images of behaviors in their minds, not just images of objects, as previously thought. From our perspective at Canine Assistants, this could open new ways of teaching and communicating with our dogs.

A few years ago, Adam wrote an article for *Current Biology* entitled "A Simple Reason for a Big Difference: Wolves Do Not Look Back at Humans, but Dogs Do." In it, he describes several experiments his team performed to evaluate the difference in the ability of dogs and wolves to communicate with people. Adam concludes, as the title suggests, that the principal reason seems to be that dogs look into people's faces when in need of help or direction, while wolves do not. Consider the story of my friend's dog, Blackie, a black Lab. Blackie is a ballplaying machine and will happily chase a tennis ball for hours. He will retrieve only the ball with which he started the game, no substitutes allowed, no matter how many are offered. So, if that ball is lost, the game is over. However, if the ball is thrown somewhere Blackie can see but cannot reach, he will work on getting it for several moments, then look back at his human pitcher, seeking assistance. If his pitcher is turned so that Blackie cannot see his face, the dog will move to make his appeal face-to-face. Blackie provides a beautiful example of the fact that dogs are both smart enough to look to people for help and astute enough to realize that they need to get people's attention in order to make a successful appeal.

It is critical that we recognize that dogs neither input nor process information exactly as humans do. Consequently, they cannot fairly be expected to think or respond as we do. That said, dogs are far more sensitive and intelligent than we may realize. The researchers who pioneered the study of animal cognition have opened the door to a better understanding of our dogs, and those like Dr. Adam Miklosi, who are following in their footsteps, are teaching us more each day.

CHAPTER SEVEN

Emotion

The request to see Dr. Nick, as the children called him, came early on a Monday. An eight-year-old boy in Phoenix had fallen off his skateboard and was clinging to life. Dr. Nick, with his old black medical bag, was on the next flight from Atlanta to Phoenix. It was my privilege to accompany him on this trip, as I had on many trips in the past. It was an experience that profoundly changed the way I understood the emotional life of dogs.

Because Nick had been trained as a service dog, he had legal access to places other dogs could not go. So, while the child's own dog was not permitted in the Phoenix hospital, Nick was welcomed. He was there on a mission so tragic it still hurts to this day. He was there to help this precious little boy die.

The child had no brain function. His stricken parents knew it was time to allow the life-sustaining machines to be turned off. The boy loved his parents mightily, but his best friend on earth was his dog. Because his dog was not allowed to be with him as he died, his parents had asked for Nick.

As soon as Nick entered the hospital room, he dropped his bag, carefully maneuvered himself around the tubes and wires, and jumped gently up onto the bed to lie quietly against the boy's side. I never gave him any direction; Nick just did what he instinctively knew to do. He stayed on the bed without moving for more than two and a half hours. Sometime during that afternoon, the boy's mother asked those of us in the room if we had put her son's arm around Nick. We told her that we had not, but indeed the child's left arm was now draped loosely across Nick's big neck. Nick had nuzzled himself there.

When the child was pronounced dead, his devastated mother broke. Her wail was unlike any noise I had ever heard. Without even seeming to displace the sweet little arm across him, Nick managed in one move to fling himself into the mother's arms. Together they stayed huddled, as if on a life raft, until the mother was led into an empty room nearby.

The nurses thanked Nick and me for coming and told us we were free to leave. In something much like shock, I stumbled to the elevator with Nick walking proudly beside me. I can remember being relieved to see that he had made it through the ordeal without too much visible trauma. But as soon as the elevator doors closed and the two of us were alone, Nick collapsed to the floor with a moan. He remained there as the elevator doors opened into the lobby. No amount of encouragement or bribery made him move. He did not look at me but rather through me, with glassy, vacant eyes. I started to worry.

With the help of a hospital intern, we carried Nick to my rental car and placed him gently on the backseat. In my heart, I felt like his reaction was one of grief, but my brain kept reminding me that he was a dog and I shouldn't anthropomorphize his response. How could he understand what had happened? If dogs are motivated only by seeking pleasure and having their own needs met, then why would Nick be so overwhelmingly sad? That little boy and his family meant nothing in terms of Nick's life.

Fearing he had suffered a stroke, I phoned a nearby veterinary clinic. A young vet helped me get Nick into a clinic exam room and, as I relayed the events of the afternoon to her, she proceeded to examine him. She found nothing wrong with him physically. He even stood up for her and finally walked with me back to the car. As the veterinarian followed us, she explained that Nick was perhaps upset because he knew I had been distressed. That would fit right in with the concept that dogs worry only about what might affect them, I thought. She explained that there really was no way to tell if a dog was truly feeling emotion. We could only describe the dog's behavior but could not speculate as to any inner feelings that might be causing the behavior.

I started to leave, not completely persuaded by her explanation but at least confident that Nick wasn't physically ill. I could see by the look on her face that she wasn't convinced by her textbook answers either. So I wasn't surprised to see her raised arm as I began to drive off, signaling me to stop. She leaned in and looked again at Nick in the backseat. Then she confided that her gut instinct was that Nick was experiencing grief for the child, the family, or both, and his behavior wasn't about his concern for me, at least not exclusively. She went on to say that I should be careful about putting him in such emotion-laden situations in the future, since he seemed to feel things so deeply. At least, she said—ever the scientist—his behavior indicated as much.

Trying to be a "true professional" when I started Canine Assistants, I was very careful not to credit dogs with any abilities or capacities not scientifically proven. I was so afraid of being perceived as an overly emotional dog person that I refused to open my mind. Well, as usual, Nick and the other dogs opened it for me. I began to realize that many things I know to be true haven't yet been proven scientifically.

Of course Nick had been sad. I knew that in my heart all along. He had *looked* sad. His body literally sagged under the weight of his grief. He may have been concerned about me too, but he was undoubtedly experiencing his own intense emotions.

Time has taught me that dogs, like humans, are emotional creatures. Just watch a dog whose beloved owner returns home from a trip—the dog jumps for joy.

Will it ever be possible for us believers to prove that dogs experience emotions? Well, yes and no. As Patricia McConnell says in her fabulous book *For the Love of a Dog,* "Emotions are slippery things." She is absolutely correct. Does your spouse have emotions? How do you know? Can you actually experience what he is experiencing internally? If not, then how can you know for certain that he has emotions? Of course, it's simple: You ask him. Therein lies the problem with animal emotions. Not only can we not experience what they experience emotionally, we can't ask them what they're feeling. However, we can exercise a little common sense.

With the rise of ethology—the study of animal behavior—scientists began to allow for what actually causes behavior: emotion. Behavior problems are the number-one cause of preventable death—euthanasia—for dogs under three years of age in the United States. Dogs have emotions. Emotions cause them to behave in certain ways. We must understand the source and catalysts of emotion before we can hope to deal successfully with behavioral problems that result from it.

Dr. McConnell explains that every emotional experience includes changes in the body, changes in expression, and thoughts or feelings that go along with them. The scenario: A man is pointing a gun at Nick as I stand next to him. The threat is real and my body floods with norepinephrine, a stress hormone that affects the part of the brain controlling action; I prepare for "fight or flight." My expression changes, my eyes widen, and my pupils dilate. I'm thinking to myself, *Oh, God, Nick is going to get shot.* I reach out and pull Nick to safety.

This simple short scene illustrates that emotions do precipitate a range of action, from subtle eye gestures to racing heartbeats to sweeping body movements. Researchers used to believe that as our senses registered something—a charging bear, for example—we would experience an emotion, and that emotion would cause changes in our body, expression, and thoughts. Some experts now speculate that that theory was backward, believing instead that as we register sensory data that causes changes to our body and mind, we then feel the fear. I see a man with a gun turn toward my beloved dog, my body chemistry changes, my eyes widen in horror, and I think, *Oh, no!* Only after all of that do I feel fear.

It is counterintuitive to claim that emotion doesn't affect animals. After all, how long would a species survive without being able to experience fear? More and more experts are starting to agree. Marc Bekoff, professor emeritus of biology at the University of Colorado–Boulder, says in his book *The Emotional Lives of Animals:* "It is bad biology to argue against the existence of animal emotions."

Darwin unquestionably believed that animals have emotions, and many experts still concur that what Darwin termed the "universal emotions" of fear, anger, disgust, surprise, sadness, and happiness are indeed the primary emotions. These are the emotions that require no conscious thought to experience, since they are born with us, hardwired into our systems.

The "triune model" from neurologist Paul MacLean suggests that we have three separate brains representing different levels of evolution. The lowest level is the reptilian brain, shared by everything from snakes and fish on up the evolutionary ladder to the very top. In addition, mammals have a paleomammalian, or limbic, brain. Finally, the more highly evolved species like man and dog have a top level known as the cerebral cortex, the thinking part of the brain that is far larger in man than in any other species. Though there may be multiple "emotion systems" in an individual's brain, primary emotions are connected to the limbic system and thus to the limbic brain shared by all mammals.

Still, some behaviorists assert that emotions are a mere reflexive process in animals other than humans. According to them, animals can experience emotions but they cannot think about them.

Accordingly, Nick could experience sadness but not grief, since that would require he understand something about life and the lack thereof. That argument is understandable—dogs do not have the same large cerebral cortex as man, and therefore some secondary emotions that involve understanding are too complex for a dog's smaller cognitive capacity. I, however, disagree that dogs are incapable of experiencing secondary emotions.

Disappointment is a secondary emotion requiring an unfulfilled expectation. In order to feel disappointed, there must be anticipation. To anticipate, one must have the capacity to think about the future; to feel disappointment, one has to realize intellectually that the anticipated event did not and will not occur. This is a relatively sophisticated concept. Yet I have never met a dog owner who does not believe their dog feels disappointment. Who hasn't seen big brown eyes looking balefully at them when an important phone call postpones a planned walk in the park? Nick had the best disappointed face ever. Big rolls of skin would droop down as he pointed his nose toward the ground. His beautiful eyes would stare at me reproachfully from under his furrowed brow. His body language spoke clearly: "You let me down."

But, conversely, did he worry about disappointing me? And if he did, did he feel remorse? Remorse and its big brother, guilt, are advanced emotions. Experiencing them necessitates an understanding of a moral code and what it means to violate that code. I think dogs can understand some of our human moral code, but only the parts that overlap with their own.

Dogs have an ancestral code of moral conduct. Wolves have strict social rules. Some of those rules are easy to identify in dogs today. For example, dogs practice the concept of possession being nine-tenths of the law—though with dogs, it is more like possession is ten-tenths of the law. The most timid member of a dog family will growl and snap even at a more dominating dog in defense of a chew bone, and the bolder dog knows better than to try to take the bone away from the one chewing it—at least not by force. Trickery, which Jack sometimes uses to take Butch's toys, seems to be acceptable. But after the bone is all gone, the more timid dog will often make gestures that acknowledge the other dog's dominance, such as face licking and submissive rolling. These actions could be considered apologetic, though they seem more likely to be an attempt to avoid later reprimand.

Dogs worry about keeping humans happy, so they go to extraordinary measures to avoid upsetting us—within the framework of their own understanding. That, though, is the limit of their capacity to experience guilt or remorse. I realize some people may disagree with me, citing examples of a dog behaving sheepishly in front of its owner before a misdeed is even discovered. Surely, they contend, this is evidence of guilt. Well, I don't believe it is, unless it pertains to some rule of conduct shared by both species. It is far more likely, for example, that the dog remembers that his owner got upset previously when he came home to find that the sofa cushions had been destroyed.

Jealousy, on the other hand, is a secondary emotion that dogs clearly experience. Remember how Jack cons Butch into leaving his toy by pretending there are people at the front door? What is at the root of that behavior for Jack if not jealousy? It is jealousy that causes one dog to bump another out of the way of your stroking hand.

Nick and I traveled a tremendous amount together, and he became a true veteran of the Atlanta International Airport, frequently cited as the busiest in the world. Due to a serious personal flaw of mine—perpetual tardiness—Nick always ran when we were in the airport. Always. We would pass through the airport doors and off we would go, a big yellow dog running, with me gracelessly trying to keep up. As we reached the security checkpoint, Nick would fling his bag (he usually carried his own luggage) onto the conveyor belt, bolt through the metal detector, and retrieve his bag on the other side. By the time Nick and I reached the underground train, I'd be a sweaty, exhausted mess.

One day I failed to hold on to the handrail, as the mechanical voice demands prior to announcing that the vehicle is leaving the station. The warning is well deserved. When I fell, my purse spilled and my stuff rolled everywhere—a truly embarrassing moment. I glanced over at Nick to make sure he was okay, since I had also dropped his leash. He was staring passively out the window of the train, some twenty feet away from me, acting as if we had never met before. It was so obvious that Nick was embarrassed by my misstep that the man who helped me up even noted, "Looks like your dog is pretending not to know you."

• • •

While dogs experience many of the same emotions as humans, they don't necessarily experience these emotions the same way that we do. I cannot tell you what Nick's exact feelings were about the death of the little boy. I can only note that he was profoundly affected emotionally by the event and that whatever he felt went far beyond simple reflex.

At Canine Assistants, I have seen many compelling examples of what can only be described as dogs grieving. It is devastatingly sad when any of our assistance dogs die. Their human partners are, of course, bereft. But somehow the people manage to keep going, to regain their balance and move on. That is not always the case when the circumstances are reversed. When working dogs lose their owners, the dogs often fall to pieces, refusing to eat or even participate in other activities of daily living. There have been anecdotal reports of service dogs who have quite literally grieved themselves to death.

The depth of their feelings suggests that the cognitive limitations of dogs may make them experience emotions much more strongly. Consider your feelings about the death of someone close to you; you are sad but you console yourself intellectually. Dogs do not appear to have that level of intellectual flexibility. When dogs feel emotion, they feel it largely without the tempering filter of higher thought.

This is an important factor when considering whether or not our dogs actually *love* us. Many people seem to think the ability to love requires a higher spirituality possessed only by humans. Consider this quote from *Chicago Tribune* columnist Eric Zorn: "To my mind, true love requires the sort of wisdom and conceptual thinking dogs are simply incapable of." In my opinion, he has it backward. It is the very wisdom of humans that makes love so difficult for us and the relative simplicity of dogs that makes their love so intense.

Unromantic as it may be, a great deal of love is chemical. Dopamine, released during pleasurable activities, causes us to feel an emotion, usually associated with falling in love. Oxytocin is the hormone that maintains those warm feelings as love matures. Oxytocin is what bonds mothers to their children. Patricia McConnell describes it as "a one-size-fits-all hormone mediating love and attachment in all social relationships that involve feelings of care and connection." From a biological standpoint, the entire process is rudimentary and well within the grasp of dogs. Their brains, too, produce the necessary dopamine and oxytocin.

Experiencing great emotion without the ability to cognitively work through it must be extremely stressful for dogs, causing emotions to run amok and creating problems such as separation anxiety. Some researchers, including McConnell, believe that dogs can suffer post-traumatic stress disorder (PTSD), wherein the memory of an emotionally traumatic event becomes itself traumatic. Those who suffer from PTSD are often hypersensitive to stimuli that are related—in even the most remote manner—to whatever caused the original trauma. This hyperreactivity stems from changes in stress hormones and in the neural pathways through which the stimulus is processed.

At Canine Assistants, a number of dogs have developed extreme hypersensitivity to noises. The problem usually begins with exposure to a startlingly loud noise, such as fireworks or balloons popping. Once the issue has been established, these dogs can become highly sensitive to even the slightest of sounds. One dog, Hershey, became so stressed by noises that the very click of the joystick on his recipient's wheelchair would send him running under the bed. Luckily, Hershey responded well to a gradual desensitizing program of medication and behavior modification, as do most other dogs.

As any veterinarian can attest, dogs can develop significant stress-related problems. Both people and dogs attempt to alleviate stress in the same manner, using what are known as displacement behaviors in order to cope. Since displacement behaviors in dogs are usually ones that humans consider misbehaviors, the more we know about stress and its effect on dogs, the better we can understand their coping processes.

There are three different categories of stress:

1. EUSTRESS is called positive stress. This is stress you can do something about. If you are excessively hungry, you feel stress. If eating satisfies that hunger, then the stress was eustress.

Eustress is positive because it helps keep us alive and encourages success.

2. NEUTRAL stress is neither positive nor negative. The television is somewhat loud, but if it doesn't bother you enough to turn it down, the stress it creates remains neutral.

3. DISTRESS is harmful stress. If you are starving and there is no way for you to get food, you are in distress. Distress has a negative impact on dogs and people both physically and mentally. The effects of distress are both immediate and long-lasting.

Since eustress is quickly resolved and neutral stress has no impact, it is distress in dogs, as it is in humans, that causes the most significant problems. There are a number of things that can affect dogs to the point of distress, including being left alone, hearing loud noises, fear of not pleasing their owners, and even boredom.

How can you tell if your dog is feeling stress? We must rely on our dogs' behaviors or, more precisely, their displacement behaviors to alert us. Common displacement behaviors in dogs include compulsively chewing on themselves or on objects, eliminating inappropriately in small amounts randomly throughout the house, obsessively digging holes outside, pacing, and chronic barking. Dogs may display these behaviors for a number of reasons, so it is important to analyze circumstances carefully to determine the cause. For example, if your dog pees a puddle by your back door, it isn't necessarily stress. It's possible he just needed to go to the bathroom and couldn't get outside.

If you are concerned that your dog is experiencing distress, it is first important to determine what emotion is causing the stress. Currently, much of dog training is focused on making a dog stop doing something we don't want him to do, without much thought given to why he is doing it in the first place. While this may provide a quick fix, it does not solve the issue for the long run. Imagine a water balloon filled to near capacity. If you keep adding water to the balloon without allowing some of the existing water to be released, the balloon will soon explode under the pressure. Now imagine that, instead of a water balloon, we are talking about a dog filled with negative stress. The displacement behaviors act like tiny pinholes, allowing some of the pressure to be reduced. If we plug the pinholes but allow stress to continue building, the dog is going to blow, somewhere, somehow. The dog may begin to chew holes in his own leg or suddenly bite for no apparent reason, or end up dying earlier than necessary. Stress has the same deleterious physical effect on dogs as it does on humans.

Figure out what is causing your dog to feel stressed and, if possible, eliminate the cause. For example, if boredom is creating stress for your dog because you must leave him alone for long periods, stop feeding him from a bowl and start stuffing his food into a Kong or similar toy, creating a long-lasting, time-occupying distraction. Mixing the food with low-fat cottage cheese and freezing it overnight can make it an even longer-lasting project. At Canine Assistants, we advise our service-dog recipients to feed their dogs in this manner, encouraging the animals to be still and quiet for extended periods of time.

If you cannot eliminate the stress, try giving your dog an alternative acceptable displacement behavior, a nondestructive pinhole. Maybe chewing on a rawhide would calm your dog even more than chewing on your shoes. Try more exercise to see if that provides him with adequate stress relief. Finally, if your dog is having a serious stress issue that you cannot seem to alleviate, take him to your veterinarian and explain the situation. If your vet doesn't seem interested or able to help with the problem, ask for a referral to a veterinary behaviorist. Don't be afraid to try medication if that is what your doctor recommends. Sometimes it is the only way to mitigate serious stress. Make no mistake, stress in your dog takes its toll. Do whatever is necessary to make your dog's life as stress-free as possible. After all, how is he going to help assuage your stress if he's busy trying to cope with his own?

Dogs are dependent upon us for their very survival, and that dependency can make them emotionally vulnerable. It is up to us to show them that we will meet their physical needs. But dogs also need to be shown that they can and do please us. Failing to assure them of that would be every bit as devastating for our dogs as failing to feed them.

CHAPTER EIGHT

Personality Plus

My sister's dog, Biscuit, was a Jack Russell terrier, like Eddie from *Frazier*. However, unlike the calm, well-trained Eddie, Biscuit was a constant ball of chaotic energy. She bounced, she pounced, she flew through the air, and she seemed never to tire of trying to escape her fenced backyard. She was pretty successful at the escaping business, being brought home by no less than her veterinarian, her groomer, the mailman, the fire department, two police cruisers, and one set of small children pulling her in a wagon. Once, when my sister's street was flooded by the overflowing Chattahoochee River, Biscuit was on the TV news, perched at the front of a rowboat being used by rescue workers to evacuate local residents. Biscuit gazed staunchly forward from the bow as if directing the rescuers' movements. She looked every bit as confident as Leonardo DiCaprio in his famous "I'm the king of the world" scene from the movie *Titanic*. Biscuit was truly one of a kind.

As my friend Gil, a Southern gentleman with a knack for stating the obvious, would have said, "Biscuit had personality plus." At least, most of us would call it "personality." There are still a few scientists who believe it is inappropriately anthropomorphic to ascribe personality to dogs. In my opinion, these scientists are stubbornly wrong.

The *American Heritage Dictionary* defines personality as "the combination of emotional, intellectual, and moral qualities that distinguishes an individual." I have often heard the terms "temperament" and "personality" used synonymously, particularly in regard to animals, but they are not the same. Temperament is the combination of the inherent characteristics with which one is born, the foundation upon which personality is built. Personality is formed through the effects of environment and experiences on one's temperament.

Dr. Samuel Gosling, a psychology professor at the University of Texas at Austin, has participated in a number of research projects on personality in dogs. Gosling, who directs UT–Austin's Animal Personality Institute, initially theorized that the idea of personality in dogs might be merely "the sentimental projections" of loving owners. Given his background in human-personality research, he decided to test his theory. In order to claim that a species had personality, specific traits had to be identified and those traits had to be measurable in a way that proved accurate no matter who gave the test. For example, Gosling would need to be able to gauge a dog's fearfulness, and everyone who assessed the dog—from his owner to his veterinarian to a total stranger—would have to come up with approximately the same answer.

In an effort to produce a valid canine-personality-assessment tool, Gosling and his colleagues began a study with several phases. In the first phase, each owner judged their dog's personality and their own. Then people who knew the owner and dog were asked to perform the same assessment of them. This allowed researchers to see how accurately owners judged their own personalities and those of their dogs. It also provided insight into the personality match between owner and dog.

In the second phase, strangers were asked to evaluate the energy level, affection, emotion, and intelligence of each dog. The evaluators watched the dogs try to get a treat from under a cup in order to get a sense of the dog's intelligence. Then they watched the dog's reaction as the owner walked away from them to get a feel for the dog's emotional reactivity. Finally, they evaluated affection by watching the dog and owner interact. Activity level was noted throughout the evaluations.

The third phase was designed to investigate whether people used stereotypes when evaluating particular dog breeds. Were the border collies all seen as brilliant and the pit bulls as vicious? In order to assess this accurately, Gosling's team found people who had no previous knowledge of the dogs being studied and asked them to evaluate personality traits based solely on photographs of the animals.

Not surprisingly, the new people did reveal breed bias in their rankings of the dogs. This information allowed Gosling to calculate a formula compensating for this predisposition, which he applied to the results of the second phase in which strangers had evaluated dogs after watching them play. Allowing for breed bias made the assessments of owners and strangers close to the same.

Gosling's work has given credence to the concept that dogs do have personalities and has encouraged further research. The ability to assess personality is critical for those of us whose job it is to place animals in certain environments, matching them with specific individuals who need assistance dogs. The greater the research, the better our results.

Some years ago, two events taught me how important it is to have a reliable method of evaluating a dog's personality and matching it to a person's. First, Nick came into my life. He fit me. He was slot A to my tab B—just perfect. I had loved other dogs before, but not as easily as I fell for Nick. Like a new bride, I was convinced that no one should have to live without the love of a good man—or, in this case, a good dog. I became the most dreaded of all friends, a "dog matchmaker." My brother, Gary, was my first target. He didn't have a dog in his life, and I sought to rectify that.

Babe, a Jack Russell mix, was an absolutely adorable dog. The young woman who owned Babe was unable to keep her, so I asked Gary if he would give Babe a home. "No," he answered. I asked again, and again, and again. Finally, he agreed.

After several weeks of living with Babe, Gary became noticeably stressed about the dog. Since he works at Canine Assistants, all his coworkers teased him about the fact that he was finding it difficult to live with Babe. "If you can't live with Babe, you can't live with any dog," one of them said. "Babe is *so* easy."

I agreed. Babe was housebroken, polite, and wasn't prone to excessive barking or any other behavioral problems. Nonetheless, you could see that the dog was driving Gary crazy, though he found it impossible to explain why. Finally, I asked if Babe could spend the night at my house so I could better understand what about the dog might be annoying.

Oh, my—what a night that was. After only two hours of Babe, I was driven absolutely nuts. The dog would not leave me alone for a second. Every step I took, she followed. When I sat, she climbed into my lap and stared into my eyes. If I took my hand off her, she pawed me until I started patting again. I knew she was nervous in a new environment, but even after settling in, Babe both gave and demanded so much affection that I could barely keep up and could hardly stand it. She spent the night in bed next to me, and on top of me, and under me, trying to find a way to burrow inside my skin. The next morning I returned Babe to my brother with great relief. I also apologized to him.

Babe taught me a very valuable lesson. I knew from Nick that matching the personality of dog and owner was helpful, but Babe taught me exactly how critical it was to the well-being of both. Clearly, my brother and I lacked the personality necessary to form a strong bond with Babe. Even with dog lovers, that happens. Babe's personality led her to behave a certain way and our personalities led us to react a certain way—not compatibly. The more agitated we became by her constant demands for reassurance, the more reassurance the poor dog needed. Thankfully, our friend Mary, one of the most nurturing people ever, was looking for a dog with whom she could do animal-assisted therapy. She adopted Babe, and they are perfect for each other. Mary radiates her adoration for the little dog day and night, and Babe is now living in a constant state of bliss.

Dr. Gosling explains that people tend to choose their dogs with a heavy emphasis on appearance and not enough focus on personality. Personality is, by far, the most important characteristic in making a strong owner-dog bond. It determines behavior, and behavior is critical to a successful relationship between man and dog. Just ask the folks who work at animal shelters why most dogs are turned in: "Behavior problems."

A study published in 2009 in the journal *Evolutionary Psychology* revealed that most of us are attracted to people who possess personality traits similar to our own. The same is true for our attraction to dogs. In simple terms, we feel the easiest and deepest connection to dogs whose personalities are just like ours.

At Canine Assistants, we extensively evaluate the personalities of both dogs and people, allowing us to tailor an appropriate education plan for each dog and, ultimately, to make better matches between dogs and people.

Using a temperament test adapted from the one initially formatted by dog trainer Wendy Volhard, we test eight principal characteristics when each puppy has reached eight weeks of age: attraction to people, willingness to follow people, retrieving interest, touch sensitivity, sound reactivity, visual reactivity, reactivity to novel stimuli, and confidence. We do this assessment to gain a general understanding of each puppy's temperament, even though such tests have not always proven to be a reliable indicator of the ultimate personality of the adult dog. A dog's experiences and environmental factors also play important roles in the development of his overall personality. However, since temperament influences a dog's perception of experience and environment, the disposition with which an individual dog is born remains the foundation of its personality. For this reason, it is important to understand each puppy's base temperament.

Most dogs are attracted to people, especially the goldens and Labs with whom we primarily work. This is something of a given, but the specific question is whether an individual puppy is confident enough to act on that attraction. To assess this, all the puppies from a litter are put into an exercise pen and then removed, one at a time. A helper—someone the puppy doesn't know—sits on the ground six feet away, calling the puppy with happy "pup-pup-puppy" noises. If the puppy scampers toward the person calling him, we know that he is attracted to human interaction. If instead the puppy runs toward his littermates in the pen, that puppy may *not* be temperamentally inclined to seek human interaction.

Once our helper has the puppy near her, she stands up and begins to walk away. We ask our helper to again make happy sounds to get the puppy's attention but then to move another ten feet or so without further effort to engage the pup. This tests whether the puppy will return to his littermates, run off to play with whatever might be available, or choose to follow the lead of a human. This is significant for our purposes. A puppy who will happily follow a human's lead shows a readiness to be taught, a particularly desirable trait for service dogs. A puppy who cares enough about people to follow them willingly, even when the comfort of his siblings is close at hand, should be an easy puppy to teach.

Next our helper shows the puppy a small stuffed animal, shaking the toy to encourage the pup's interest in it. She then tosses the toy a few feet away and watches the dog's reaction. Some puppies bound after the toy, grab it, and run away. Some grab the toy, lie down, and begin the process of ripping its stuffing out. Some show no interest in chasing the toy at all, preferring to eat sticks or play with pinecones. But a few fetch the toy and return it to the helper. These are the puppies we love to see—interested in playing but even more interested in continued interaction with humans.

Our helper then sits back on the ground and holds the puppy in her lap. After a moment of relaxing the puppy with pats, our helper holds a paw and applies steady pressure between the dog's toes with her thumb and forefinger. She isn't pinching or squeezing hard, but she is applying enough force to be felt. We time how long it takes before the dog tries to withdraw his paw. Most puppies will allow the exercise for several seconds before protesting. When we find a puppy who immediately yanks his paw away, we know he is extremely sensitive to touch, which may affect his later learning and working life. When we have a puppy who never tries to pull his paw away, we check his pulse.

After giving the puppy a few minutes to play, someone positioned behind him loudly bangs a metal spoon against a pot. Some puppies will immediately locate the source of the sound and run toward it. Others will turn to the sound but will not go toward it. Those who are innately fearful of loud noises will scamper quickly away from the banging. Dogs who are nervous about loud noises can easily develop full-fledged noise phobias, a decided problem for service dogs, so this is a temperament trait that we work hard to mitigate.

Next, a string is tied around a stuffed toy duck, and the helper pulls it slowly across the puppy's line of sight. Some puppies see the duck but do not react, some chase the duck playfully, while others pounce on the duck and try to shred it as if their life depended on it. When we have a "pouncer," we know this pup reacts very strongly to visual stimuli. Since we do not want an assistance dog who bolts after squirrels or ducks, we try to tone down this response as part of the puppy's educational development.

The next evaluation checks the young dog's reaction to novel stimuli. Our helper quickly opens a large, colorful golf umbrella directly in front of the puppy. Once again, there are several reactions: Some tentatively sniff the umbrella and then settle into reluctant acceptance of the new object; some run away; a few accept the umbrella with seemingly no concerns. The latter reaction is the one I most like to see. An assistance dog has legal access to all public places, with the exception of sterile environments such as operating and delivery rooms. A puppy who processes new things without hesitation makes our job considerably easier.

The final evaluation tests the puppy's confidence. We ask each young dog to complete a puppy-sized obstacle course consisting of a slide, a plastic tunnel, and a small swinging bridge. Our helper encourages each puppy with the promise of treats but uses no force or physical manipulation. Some of the puppies refuse to climb on or through anything; they lie down and stare at the playground from a safe distance. Others, once again, run off to play with sticks or balls or whatever distractions might be readily available. But then there are those who go barreling down the slide, bolting through the tube, and dashing across the swinging bridge as if it were as easy as an evening stroll. It is fascinating to watch how differently puppies from the same litter react. This test, like the others, gives important insight into the makeup of each individual puppy.

Understanding an individual dog's temperament allows us to develop an educational plan that will strengthen desirable characteristics and mitigate undesirable ones. For example, we had a puppy named Peaches whose assessment indicated that she was shy and fearful of novel stimuli. So we focused on getting Peaches out into the world to see new sights and sounds at least four times a week, more than normal for an eight-week-old puppy. We also concentrated on her agility work, such as walking up a ramp, going down a slide, jumping through hoops, and walking on different surfaces. Agility exercises not only improve dogs' physical well-being, they increase confidence levels. In turn, self-confidence decreases shyness and fearfulness. By the time Peaches was sixteen weeks old, she was as bold and outgoing as any of her siblings.

In addition to tailoring individual educational plans, we make certain each puppy has significant exposure to those things he might encounter in his life as an assistance dog, such as wheelchairs, walkers, chairlifts, elevators, escalators, and loud traffic noises. Additionally, we attempt to increase his confidence both in his own abilities and in the capability and reliability of his handler. Building trust in humans is an integral part of our educational process. As a puppy encounters new things in his life, he must realize his human partner will always be there, willing and able to help if needed.

As our dogs approach one year of age, their personalities are still something of a work in progress, so each is reevaluated by the primary handler. This allows us to check our efforts in strengthening or mitigating temperamental traits. We use a personality analysis called the Canine Behavior Type Index, or CBTI for short, developed by

Kenneth Dagley, a trainer, and Dr. Jacqueline Perkins, a veterinarian, from the GOOD DOG Behaviour Clinics in Australia.

The CBTI measures three different dimensions of personality. First, the Environmental Dimension assesses whether the dog is more of an organized type or a spontaneous type. The organized types like a place for everything and everything in its place. These dogs are "team players," most likely to be herders. Spontaneous types, on the other hand, don't care much about the big picture, preferring to focus on whatever has captured their interest at any given instant.

Next, the Social Dimension uses a linear hierarchy of alpha, beta, and gamma classifications to chart the dog's social position and willingness to follow social rules. Alphas are confident and controlling. Betas tend to challenge their place in the social order, the quintessential social climbers. Gammas are followers, following both the lead of others and the rules of social conduct.

Finally, the Motivational Dimension measures how "intense" a dog is. Dogs are classified as either high or medium energy. Energy in this case refers not only to how playful and bouncy the dogs are but also to how willing they are to exert the effort needed to accomplish a task, like herding sheep or retrieving objects. Medium levels of intensity in this category tend to moderate the behavioral effects of the other two dimensions, while high levels tend to amplify them.

Based on these three areas of evaluation, each dog is classified into one of twelve profiles: the Commando, the Director, the Defender, the Sentry, the Deputy, the Diplomat, the Rebel, the Aristocrat, the Adventurer, the Dreamer, the Investigator, and the Companion. CBTI provides a brief description of how best to handle dogs that fall within each profile. This interesting test, which provides owners with useful details about their dogs, is available free of charge to anyone at www.petconnectgame.com.

At Canine Assistants, as we prepare to match graduating dogs with recipients, we conduct one final evaluation of their personalities using our own adaptation of Wilson Learning's system of personality assessment. A brilliant woman and wonderful friend, Dr. Bonnie Bergin of the Bergin University of Canine Studies, introduced us to this method. Bonnie figured out that the assessment, though initially designed for people, works for dogs as well. We also use the test to evaluate the applicants who are slated to come to the next training camp to receive a dog. This way we are able to compare the personalities of both dog and person on the same scale. This comparison is vital to making the most-effective placements. For example, recipients should be more assertive than their dogs so that control does not become an issue; conversely, dogs should be slightly more social so that their owners always feel loved.

The assessment is made through a series of surveys completed by five different people who have worked closely with the dog being evaluated. The survey lists statements such as "is warm," "is reliable," "is loyal," and "is adaptable"; evaluators rate the accuracy of each statement in describing the dog with a numerical response between 1 and 7—1 being you strongly agree and 7 being you strongly disagree. The calculated results of each of the five surveys are averaged to provide a numerical score for the dog's assertiveness, sociability, and adaptability. The same process applies to impending recipients, using friends and family to complete the surveys.

The results of sociability and assertiveness calculations are plotted on a graph, which is divided into four main sections or personality types (see chart on p. 99).

After determining the primary personality of a given individual, we go a step further and determine the secondary, or backup, personality type. Secondary personality type is particularly important for us at Canine Assistants since Labs and goldens, the breeds we principally use, are Amiable in primary personality type. Therefore, we often match the secondary personality type of a dog with the primary personality type of the recipient. We have found this works extremely well, since it allows us to follow the principle that a dog should be more social and less assertive than his recipient.

In addition to calculating sociability and assertiveness, we measure versatility, the ability to adapt one's behavior to better meet the needs of another. Versatility can be gauged numerically from 0 to 28 and the results plotted along a straight line. The more versatile an individual—whether human or canine—the more capable they are of

ANALYTICALS
- Not very social or assertive
- Have serious facial expressions, often with a furrowed brow
- Slow, precise, and methodical, as they do not like to make mistakes
- Prefer to keep touching to a minimum
- Do not like to take risks

DRIVERS
- Highly assertive but not very social
- Often appear to be leaning forward even when standing still
- Tightly controlled and driven to succeed
- Do not like physical contact
- Willing to take risks when the payoff is substantial

AMIABLES
- Highly social but not very assertive
- Warm and friendly
- Forgiving and easygoing
- Enjoy physical contact
- Do not like to take risks
- Like to concentrate on one thing at a time—usually smelling the roses

EXPRESSIVES
- Highly assertive and highly social
- Like to be the center of attention
- Creative, charismatic, and funny
- Impatient and informal
- Enjoy physical contact
- Willing to take risks

handling new people and situations. They can fit in anywhere, with anyone, and they are chameleonlike in their capacity to model their behavior to make those around them feel comfortable. Great hostesses and salespeople are undoubtedly highly versatile. On the other end of the scale, those who are not very versatile find it difficult to adapt to anything outside their established routine and have trouble matching their behavior to the needs of others.

Here's an example, using Nick and me, that illustrates the versatility scale:

```
0_____|_____|24_____|28
                                          Nick    Me
```

Nick was a 20 on the scale and I was a 24, meaning that together we were extremely versatile.

I suspect that Amiables and Expressives are likely to be more versatile overall than Analyticals and Drivers; the more socially comfortable the individual, the more easily he or she can adapt to different circumstances. Versatility allows an individual to step, for a brief time, outside the behavior traits associated with his given personality in order to meet the needs of others. It doesn't, however, mean an Expressive will be comfortable acting like an Analytical for an extended period, or vice versa.

One of the most important aspects of my job is the matching of recipient and dog. Bringing home a new dog, particularly an assistance dog, is much like bringing home a new spouse: both thrilling and terrifying. If you don't start off in a state of blissful adoration, you will be checking out the return policy long before your first anniversary. It is my responsibility to be sure that our recipients and dogs begin their lives together cushioned against those early bumps by strong mutual attraction and affection.

For the first two days of our two-week training camp, my staff and I look on as recipients work with several dogs we have preselected for them based on personality. We are watching carefully to see which dog seems to be the most attracted to which individual. At the end of the second day, we ask the recipients to make a list of the dogs with whom they felt most comfortable. The staff and I then review our notes along with the recipients' requests and make the final matches. Most recipients end up with their first choice, and though not every match works, nearly 90 percent of those made at Canine Assistants are still going strong one year later.

I must confess that, for all our analysis, the staff and I have surprisingly little to do with making the matches between dog and recipient. In fact, the recipients themselves have little to do with making the matches. How does it happen? The *dogs* pick their people. A dog may be scheduled to work with four different recipients over the first two days. After giving the first three minimal attention and almost no work, he then meets the fourth and the lights come on and bells start ringing. The dog literally transforms. Suddenly, he has eyes only for that one person.

Jorge was a yellow Lab trained at Canine Assistants who I despaired would ever find his recipient match. Jorge went through four training camps, working with twenty-three different people, ignoring them all, and doing none of the tasks he had been taught. Then he met a little girl named Emma. Immediately, he climbed into her lap, licking her as if the two were long-lost best friends just reunited. He did everything the six-year-old girl asked him to do. He sat, he downed, he rolled, he retrieved, and he comported himself like an obedience champ. Needless to say, Emma put Jorge at the top of her list.

For obvious reasons, virtually every recipient requests the dog that clearly has already selected her or him. Maggie, a small golden, chose Rob the moment she placed her front paws gently into the young boy's fragile lap. Though other dogs responded to Rob's cues more quickly, Maggie alone cast a spell over him—Rob wanted only Maggie. As a matter of fact, we made a permanent change to our matching schedule because of this young man. Rob met Maggie on Monday, the first day of camp. When training was over for the day and the recipients were ready to head back to their hotel for the night, Rob refused to leave Maggie, lying down next to her kennel. Finally, his mom had to carry him away as he sobbed. Rob was terrified that he wouldn't be given Maggie when we announced the matches on Wednesday. I will never forget the look of love and anguish on that child's face as his mother pulled him away from Maggie that first evening. No one wanted Rob to spend another night worrying, so we announced the matches on Tuesday rather than Wednesday, something we have done ever since. When I announced that Maggie was going to Rob, the child fainted in his wheelchair, overcome with excitement.

Why did Maggie connect to Rob so strongly and so quickly? In part it is because dogs feel the most comfortable with people who have personality types similar to their own; Maggie and Rob nearly overlapped each other on the personality grid. But it seems to go beyond the realm of personality and into something that can be described only as "chemistry." It is obvious when the dog feels the connection as Maggie did with Rob. You can see it in their eyes—and you can see it in their tails.

A great deal can be determined about the mood, and even the overall personality, of dogs by evaluating how they carry and wag their tails. Expressive dogs carry their tails high and wag them in big circles like a helicopter's rotor. Amiables tend to carry their tails in a relaxed position with the tip pointed down, wagging in sweeping side-to-side movements that often wiggle their whole hind end. Maggie, like her little boy, Rob, is an Amiable–Amiable, and on matching day, her tail wagged so hard and wide, it appeared her whole rear end came up off the ground. Analyticals tend to carry their tails tightly against their bodies and wag them in a short, tentative arc. Likewise, Drivers usually wag their tails only within their body frame, though you will often see them carrying their tails higher than those of Amiables or Analyticals.

Dogs who are happy and comfortable wag their tails with more abandon than do dogs who are stressed. But dogs who are stressed *do* wag their tails sometimes, albeit usually in small, tight motions. Never consider a dog safe to approach simply because his tail is wagging. Tails give important information on the state of the dog, but that information must be evaluated in the context of the dog as a whole. It is difficult for me to watch fear-based trainers work with dogs, as invariably the dogs wag their tails, if at all, in pacification— a close arc that keeps the top of the tail clamped tightly to the body in an effort at self-protection. I will never understand how any so-called "trainer" would see the instillation of terror as an effective teaching tool.

Nick, feeling no fear, wagged his tail in a huge circular motion as he worked. As a matter of fact, he was so bold that we have seen only one human and no dogs chart more assertive than he did. Nick was an Expressive–Expressive. Guess who else's personality-type test was Expressive–Expressive? You got it—mine. No wonder we loved each other so quickly and with so much intensity. We were very much alike. Now, sixteen years later, my current best dog friend,

Jack, was evaluated as an Analytical–Expressive. He isn't quite as social or as assertive as Nick. Yet I still feel a deep connection with him, though the connection took some time to develop. Recently, I was trying to decide whether that was because I see some of Nick in him, making him especially dear to me, or that we are close enough in personality for it to still be a good match.

My husband suggested that I take the personality test again. "You've changed some since the early days," he told me.

"Maybe," I answered. He was correct. This time my assessment came back Analytical–Expressive. What does that mean? Had I mellowed with age? Does the fact that I now spend time writing merely make me seem less social? Or, in the four years I have spent with Jack, has my personality become more like his?

I would suspect that rather than starting out with similar personalities, as did Nick and I, Jack and I have influenced each other's personality over time. Certainly, the longer we have lived together, the better the communication between us has become. If indeed our personalities have morphed over time, perhaps that accounts in some measure for our increased mutual understanding. Whatever the cause, he and I have become fluent in the language of each other. It is, for us, a language of love.

CHAPTER NINE

Language

Bud was in training at Canine Assistants to be a seizure response dog, and he was a double handful. He was a mixed breed, a true "Georgia Brown," as we call them, who'd been adopted from a local animal shelter. Smart as a whip and too perceptive for his own good, Bud had his trainers sweating to keep up with him. He taught himself tricks such as escaping from his kennel, nabbing treats off the top shelf, and pickpocketing unsuspecting visitors. His wild-dog days came to a crashing halt, however, the day he met Trey, a boy who needed him desperately. The bond was immediate and clear. It was as if Bud understood that his impetuous youth was behind him and that he now had a serious job to do. There were many tears from staff members as Bud walked proudly beside Trey to accept their diploma from service-dog school. Bud, the most beloved bad boy of all bad boys, had made it.

Several days after graduation, Trey's mother, Beth, called; she was "very upset" about Bud. Beth sobbed out her fear that she had taken on too much. I held my breath, waiting to hear how bad Bud had been. "Bud acted like a crazy man," Beth cried. "He was tugging on

Trey and trying to pull him down. He just wouldn't leave him alone. And poor Trey had a grand mal seizure while Bud was pulling on him."

As one of my friends from North Carolina would say, "Hello, Lavenia!" Bud was not misbehaving—he was alerting to the oncoming seizure in the only way he knew! Though Bud had been trained to respond by getting help when an episode occurred, it was unclear how he would react with Trey if he began to predict his seizures. Dogs often have different methods of alerting for different people and in different situations. During training, Bud's response was gentle and subdued, but his alert with Trey was much more frantic. Tugging patients toward the ground is a common and seemingly instinctual reaction in most seizure-alert dogs, as if the dogs understand—even dogs who have never witnessed a seizure—that the patient might fall and be injured. Bud was trying to express himself in the only way he knew—through his actions. What we had was a classic "failure to communicate." Once Beth understood the reason for Bud's frantic behavior, she was absolutely blown away, as she should have been. Thereafter, Bud never failed to sense Trey's oncoming seizures, and his ability to give advance warning most certainly saved Trey's life on at least two occasions—once by attempting to pull Trey out of a pool when he sensed an attack coming and another time by physically blocking Trey's path so that he couldn't cross the street when he was about to have a seizure.

Miscommunications are common among members of our own species. Add another species to the mix and you have the potential for significant, even catastrophic, misunderstandings. Communication is the ability to present information to others in a way that is understandable and the ability to understand information being presented. In order to communicate effectively, one's efforts must consistently mean the same thing, taking context into consideration. These consistent efforts form a language.

In the *American Heritage Dictionary,* language is defined as "communication of thoughts and feelings through a system of arbitrary signals, such as voice sounds, gestures, or written symbols." It further defines language as "the manner or means of communication between living creatures other than humans." While these are not scientific definitions, they will make our discussion easier. The question of what constitutes a language remains in the hands of linguists, but for the purposes of this book I am calling "the organized communications of dogs" a language.

Language can be productive (originating the communication) or receptive (comprehension of the communication of another). The productive language of dogs is rich and multifaceted, consisting of various vocalizations, facial expressions, odor secretions, and intricate body positions and movements. In addition, dogs are extraordinarily skilled at receptive language. Many—myself among them—would claim that we do not understand our dogs' communications, especially their nonverbal ones, nearly as well as they understand ours.

Barks, growls, whines, whimpers, squeaks, yips, and howls are part of all canids' vocal language. Wolves use a gruff-sounding bark to defend their dens or to warn others, including pups, to watch their step. Wolves don't truly howl at the moon, but they do howl to summon pack members after a long hunt or in dense woods where visual contact is limited. Studies by wolf expert David Mech indicate that packs also howl more when they have a fresh kill or a new den of puppies, seemingly offering a warning to other packs to keep their distance. It appears that wolves sometimes howl out of sheer excitement. Also, wolves will howl back at the howling of others, even that of humans.

As much as wild canids vocalize, domestic dogs speak even more. In 2000, Christian-Albrechts-University in Kiel, Germany, released the results of a study that compared the barks of eighty-four dogs from nine different breeds. The results indicated that domestic dogs use vocalizations to express a variety of needs and emotions, including fear, pain, anxiety, and joy.

In a separate study, Dr. Karen Overall of the University of Pennsylvania School of Veterinary Medicine's behavior clinic examined the barks of thirty different dogs to determine if there were differences in the sound waves produced in varying situations. According to the study, the sounds of dogs not feeling stress were melodious, while the sounds of a dog under stress or in distress were high-pitched and strident. Dr. Overall said, "The single biggest underappreciated part of dog behavior is that much of what dogs do is about soliciting information. They want confirmation of what is happening or want to test a hypothesis. Barking is a means of doing that." Our dogs also use barking in an effort to communicate relevant information to humans.

Nick wasn't a big barker until someone he didn't recognize got within fifty feet of our house. When that happened, he would let loose the most frightening barrage of barking you have ever heard. I had already learned that the best way to quiet Nick was to acknowledge that he was giving me information and then tell him how I felt about the matter. The usual scenario went something like this: A man would walk by the gate to our yard, and Nick, watching out our front window, would begin to bark ferociously. I would say, "Oh, is there someone out there?" as I went to peer out the window myself. As soon as I saw that the man was no threat, I would tell Nick as much, in a calm, relaxed voice, and his barking would cease.

One day, though, when I looked out the window, I wasn't certain everything was okay. A man had stopped in front of our gate and was looking very strangely at the house. As I watched, he vaulted the fence and started down our driveway. "He's not okay," I told Nick, who had quieted as soon as I took over the lookout duties. Nick, hearing the strain in my tone, again began his vicious barking. The man stopped dead in his tracks for a moment and then turned and ran. I think his feet left the ground about ten feet before he actually reached the fence, but he cleared it at a height I judged to be approximately terror plus two feet. The man continued running down the street.

I never was able to determine why the man was coming down our driveway or what his plans might have been. For all I knew, he might have run out of gas nearby or been in need of directions, but he made me uneasy and I was glad Nick chased him away. I have no idea whether the man knew anything about dogs; however, he clearly understood what Nick was saying.

While, under most circumstances, we may not enjoy the sound of barking, dogs have much to articulate. What do our dogs mean when they vocalize? In 2003, Dr. Norio Kogure, a PhD in veterinary medicine from the Kogue Animal Hospital in Tokyo, Japan, released an invention known as the Bow-Lingual, a machine housed in a small box that translates a dog's barks into human language. Kogure tested the barks of more than eighty breeds in order to create a template that categorized barks into six groups: happiness, sadness, anger, desire, frustration, and assertiveness. From there, the device can select from the more than two hundred words recorded to more specifically identify the bark's meaning, producing phrases such as, "You're ticking me off." The device can also record barks for up to twelve hours to capture a dog's feelings when left alone for an extended period.

But do we really need a translator? Some dog sounds are easy to identify, such as Nick's threatening bark or the low, menacing tone of a "back off" growl. In fact, vocalizations of dogs are one communication form humans seem to read well. Ethologist Peter Pongracz conducted a study in 2005 that concluded that humans are able to distinguish between barks of aggression, fearfulness, and playfulness. Further studies done by Pongracz have indicated that children can differentiate between barks, suggesting that we may be born with this ability. A few researchers have speculated that some dogs' vocalizations are an effort to mimic humans, since we are such a verbal species.

These studies, among others, have established that there is motive and meaning behind a dog's bark. With this in mind, there are better ways to deal with our dogs' barking than by aversive means such as shock collars, citronella-spray collars, and squirt bottles filled with vinegar. Perhaps we should make more of an effort to figure out *why* a dog is barking. It seems far easier to stop a dog from barking if you have some idea of why he is barking in the first place.

• • •

Whether dogs will ever be able to speak as humans do seems im-plausible, even cartoonish, but such a staggering concept should not be ruled out completely. We know that the capacity for speech evolved in man over a very long period of time. Neanderthals did not have the ability to speak as precisely as we do today because they lacked our elongated trachea and our supralaryngeal vocal tract. As a child grows, his tongue gradually descends into the pharynx and changes shape, which makes precision speech possible. Dogs are far younger creatures on the evolutionary scale than are humans. Where will evolution lead them?

As the human brain evolved, it increased in size, allowing for the development of linguistic skills. However, that growth also displaced many of the sensory receptors early man had for smell, causing us to lose our acute olfactory capability. This process began to take place less than 150,000 years ago, at about the same time that some re-searchers believe the first dogs evolved from wolves. What can dogs do far better than humans? Smell. Was the super-olfactory ability of dogs coincidental to the development of the human–dog relation-ship? Or was it among the reasons for the relationship? Some scien-tists suggest that the olfactory skills of dogs allowed human linguistic ability to develop, as humans began to use domesticated dogs as their smell detectors.

Knowing how well dogs can smell, it makes sense that odor would be an important part of canine communication. We have all seen dogs mark their territory as they take their nightly walk. Most of the communication based on odor is inaccessible to humans, with our relatively poor sense of smell, but excretion is the most prevalent form of scent language used by dogs. We have also seen dogs sniffing where others have marked. Dogs are able to receive a remarkable amount of information from reading pee-mail, such as who's in heat and who's not feeling well. Some researchers even believe that dogs may be able to tell the age of the dog who has scented a particular area.

Dogs use their sense of smell to gain information in other ways too. Every night when my husband, Kent, the staff veterinarian for Canine Assistants, comes home from the clinic, Butch spends a good two or three minutes sniffing him from shoes to hat. I am convinced that Butch keeps a running record of which dogs have been in for annual visits, which dogs are sick, and, as Butch is a stud dog, which females might be looking for a good time.

Why do dogs love rolling in stinky stuff? This is likely a lupomorphic characteristic that dogs still possess. Scent is the wolf's primary form of communication. Wolves use scent to share communal information, including the location of food sources, with their pack-mates and pups. David Mech tells a story in his book *The Way of the Wolf* about watching a mother wolf feed on the carcass of a musk ox. After eating for a while, the female headed back to her den, where pack members and puppies met her with great enthusiasm. She patiently allowed each wolf to get a good sniff of her and then regurgitated part of her meal for her pups to eat. After smelling the female and carefully studying the proceedings for a short while, the pack's alpha male set out to scent the mother wolf's route home from the musk ox carcass for a meal of his own. He seemingly copied her course perfectly. So when your dog returns from a romp in the woods covered in a noxious odor, he may just be trying to let you know where he has been—and that food might be available!

My dog Jack loves to bring back a scent record of all that he has encountered while he has been outside. I never cease to be amazed at the amount of dead and rotting items he can uncover in our yard—and that our yard is the burial ground for such an extraordinary number of creatures. Jack delights in sharing these odors with me.

Dogs, like their wolf ancestors, also seem to mark territory to alert others of their presence and to leave an olfactory trail for themselves. While urine is the primary marker, feces are also effective. The anal glands secrete an intensely strong-smelling addition to the feces during and after excretion.

Body language is the principal form of productive language for dogs. They use their bodies to communicate with other canines and with humans. Since there are a limited number of movements and postures dogs can produce, many are used with minor (or no) variations to mean different things in different contexts. For example, a dog assuming a bowing position with his torso and his tail down is probably issuing an invitation to play with another dog, whereas the torso bow with his tail up likely means "I'm about to pounce on you, so get ready to play!" Remember to look at the whole dog, rather than just one part, and consider the context when trying to decipher your dog's body language.

Once you understand your dog's body language, you will find that he communicates nonstop. Learning to recognize your dog's signals and gestures is easy if you simply focus on what I call communication "hot spots." These hot spots are the corners of the mouth where the lips meet (known as the commissure), the tail (especially the base), the ears, and the eyes. Studying these spots will provide a good idea of a dog's current state. For additional confirmation, check the other important body indicators, such as the face, the torso, and the legs and paws. Dogs frequently lift a paw up toward their owner when unsure of what is being asked of them, indicating a desire to please. This is a gesture I call "the paw of appeasement." Here are some other commonly expressed phrases by dogs, including a review of the hot spots and additional indicators.

"I'm a happy dog."

HOT SPOTS:

The commissure is relaxed. The mouth itself is probably open, but even if it is closed, the lips are loose.

The base of the tail is not at all clinched. The tail itself is quite likely to be wagging.

The ears may be pricked up a bit in expectation of more good things coming or may be down and relaxed.

The eyes are soft, with no tension in the brows.

ADDITIONAL INDICATORS:

Wrinkling in the face, but the wrinkles are soft and loose, much like the wrinkles humans get when smiling.

The torso appears normal, with no sign of abdominal tucking or rounding in the back.

"I love you."

HOT SPOTS:

The commissure may be relaxed, with the mouth open, or tilted up in just a hint of a smile.

The entire tail is loose.

The ears are relaxed.

The eyes are soft and shiny. The shininess of eyes is, in large part, the result of the tear film, which is spread by blinking. There is some evidence that dopamine, a hormone associated with love, causes increased spontaneous blinking, giving eyes that extra shine.

ADDITIONAL INDICATORS:

The face may be wrinkled with happiness, but there are no visible ridges.

The torso is relaxed.

A paw lifted in appeasement if the dog feels at all uncertain about his ability to please you.

"I'm relaxed."

HOT SPOTS:

Relaxed, loose lips.

No tension in the tail.

Soft eyes.

Ears relaxed.

ADDITIONAL INDICATORS:

No ridges in the face.

No muscular tension in the torso. If lying down, the dog is rolled over on one hip. The breathing pattern is steady, with an occasional sigh of contentment.

One paw loosely tucked in.

"Let's play."

HOT SPOTS:

Lips open or lightly closed.

Tail held up, unless dog is in a play bow.

Eyes are somewhat widened.

Ears are perked up.

ADDITIONAL INDICATORS:

Furrowing of eyebrows.

The dog's whole body is tilted toward you.

Paws dancing in short steps.

"What in the world is that?"

HOT SPOTS:

Lips lightly compressed.

Tail aloft with slight tension.

Eyes slightly widened.

Ears unevenly perked.

ADDITIONAL INDICATORS:

Brows furrowed.

Body tilted slightly toward the object of curiosity, unless the dog is frightened, in which case the body will be shifted backward in preparation for a quick getaway.

A paw held up toward the object of curiosity.

Piloerection, or raised hackles, if the dog is fearful.

"I'm anxious."

HOT SPOTS:

Lips clamped and pulled back or open with spatulated tongue. "Spatulate" is the term used to describe a tongue that looks so wide at the end you think it couldn't possibly fit back into the dog's mouth.

Tail tucked in protection of vulnerable areas.

Eyes narrowed.

Ears up and back.

ADDITIONAL INDICATORS:

Face is ridged with tension.

Body slightly tucked up, as if the dog is sucking in its stomach.

Back rounded.

Piloerection.

Legs braced.

"I'm very afraid."

HOT SPOTS:

Lips pulled back and tightly compressed or pulled back in a snarl.

Tail is either completely tucked or held rigidly aloft.

Eyes are wide with much white visible, in a position known as "whale eye."

Ears are down and back.

ADDITIONAL INDICATORS:

Face is ridged with tension.

Piloerection.

Body cowering or held rigidly still. *Note: When dogs go completely and oddly still for a brief instant, they are very likely to bite.*

Legs are rigidly braced. A paw may be lifted in appeasement.

All of these indicators could easily be followed by a bite, so be careful when approaching or working with a dog who exhibits these extreme signs of fear.

"I don't understand what you want, but I'm trying."

HOT SPOTS:

Lips lightly compressed.

Tail may be wagging tentatively.

Eyes focused intently on you or looking downward.

Ears are up and back.

ADDITIONAL INDICATORS:

Face creased with tension.

Tight torso muscles.

A paw lifted in appeasement.

"Please don't be mad."

HOT SPOTS:

Lips pulled back; may be turned up in a big grin. *Note: Smiles aren't always a sign of submission. We have a Canine Assistants dog who smiles virtually all the time, except when he is nervous.*

Tail is down.

Eyes are upwardly focused on you.

Ears are down.

ADDITIONAL INDICATORS:

Face creased with tension.

Body lowered toward the ground.

A paw lifted in appeasement.

These are all signs that your dog is most distressed. Accept his apology; it is being sincerely offered.

"The cat, not me, is responsible for this calamity."
HOT SPOTS:

Lips are compressed with disapproval over the cat's irresponsibility.

Tail is tucked slightly, in deference to the likelihood that the cat will take a swipe at any exposed body parts.

Eyes are rolled up in disgust.

Ears are alert to any sound of rewards for having identified the responsible party.

ADDITIONAL INDICATORS:

Face shows marked tension ridges, caused by merely having to live with a cat.

Stomach is tucked in, due to nausea that you will think he is the guilty party.

Paw is rigidly extended in a point directly at the cat.

All dogs, whether they live with a cat or not, have stress in their lives. One way in which dogs cope with this is through an interesting form of body language called calming or cutoff signals. Dogs use calming to relax themselves and others in situations that they find difficult or frightening. Watch your dog when something unusual is going on around the house, and you should see some of the signals:

- A yawn when it isn't sleep time.
- Lip licking when no food is present.
- Rapid blinking or squishing of the eyes.
- The overwhelming need to be certain that all personal parts are still in place. Officially known as the urogenital check.
- The discovery of a fascinating scent in the opposite direction of whatever is making the dog nervous.
- Taking a "time-out" to scratch. (Canine Assistants dogs occasionally seem irritated by the packs they wear for identifi-

cation, scratching at them when working in public. After studying the problem, I realized that scratching was a calming signal.)

- Shaking off as if thoroughly wet.

Another type of body language frequently seen in dogs is eye movement used to direct another individual's gaze, a process known as gaze redirection. Nick was an expert at directing my vision by staring first at me and then at whatever he wanted me to see. He was extremely tenacious in his effort to redirect my gaze and never failed to focus me on the desired object. This amazing ability always left me with warm feelings about the closeness of our relationship. Nick also seemed to enjoy the experience, since the most-common objects toward which he directed my gaze contained food, and he generally got what he wanted.

Tails play an important part in canine communication. A 2007 study conducted at the University of Trieste in Italy, by a research team consisting of a neuroscientist and several veterinarians, found that dogs wag their tails more to the left when they are fearful or anxious and more to the right when they are attracted to something or happy. It has long been known that, in humans, the left side of the brain is associated with positive feelings, like love, safety, and attachment, and the right side of the brain with feelings of fear and depression. Because the right side of the brain controls the left side of the body and vice versa, unhappiness is often easier to read on the left side of the human face and happiness is more easily seen on the right side.

In order to determine how a dog's tail would reflect this type of emotional asymmetry, the research team studied thirty pet dogs volunteered by local families. With cameras monitoring the process, the dogs were put into fully enclosed cages that had slits in the front through which they could see. The dogs were then shown separately their owners, a stranger, a sweet cat, and an extremely aggressive dog. The results showed:

- When the dogs saw their owners, the dogs' tails wagged farther to the right than to the left, indicating positive emotions from the left side of the brain.
- When the dogs saw the stranger or the friendly cat, their tails again wagged farther to the right than to the left, though not to such a pronounced degree as when seeing their owners.
- When the dogs saw the aggressive dog, their tails wagged more toward the left than the right, indicating negative, or right brain, emotions.

Dr. Lesley Rogers, a neuroscientist at the University of New England in Australia, believes that having a brain divided into two different sides for "okay" and "dangerous" is an ancient trait that gives a species a survival advantage, allowing them to do two things at the same time, such as eat and watch for predators. Until recently, many scientists maintained that only humans had left-right-side brain asymmetry.

I don't know a dog owner who doesn't admit to talking to their dog, but how many words of human language can our dogs understand? The answer probably depends on the dog. Rico, the German border collie, proved that he knew the names of more than two hundred objects. Other studies have confirmed that dogs can understand some words of human language. Many of us have to spell out in a whisper, "I am g-o-i-n-g for a r-i-d-e in the c-a-r," lest we find Fido already buckled into the passenger's seat. So we already know that our dogs understand some of our words, but people often notice that the tone in which a word is said seems to have more impact on the dog than the word itself. This is most certainly true. No matter how smart dogs are, human speech just isn't their thing. The tone in which words are spoken takes on a greater meaning, just as it would if we were in a foreign country and didn't speak the language.

Ask any dog trainer and he will tell you it's far easier to teach a dog a behavior by using a hand signal than by using a spoken word. Why? Because dogs can easily read our body language. For cen-

turies, dogs have been carefully watching people in order to understand and anticipate their movements. This close scrutiny most likely
started in an effort to get the most food, avoid danger, and ensure
that they stayed on humans' good side. Evolutionary anthropologist
Brian Hare speculates that the ability to read human body language
was one of the traits selected when dogs were being domesticated.
In other words, dogs that were better at reading people were more
likely to be nurtured by humans and therefore had the opportunity
to reproduce successfully.

The seizure response dogs trained by Canine Assistants were fea-
tured in an amazing *National Geographic* television special called *Dog
Genius*. The show also investigated several research projects at the
Max Planck Institute in Germany, which indicated that dogs are far
better than even chimpanzees at following a human's pointed finger
to find hidden food. Non-dog-owning scientists were shocked by
the fact that a dog would consider any gesture made by a human important, when it was quite clear that the chimpanzees did not. Those
of us who have dogs were surprised that the scientists were shocked!
Of course dogs can follow your pointed finger to hidden food.
Researchers at Max Planck also found that dogs could follow a
human's gaze when they looked at the container under which food
was hidden. The human face is capable of producing a myriad of expressions, including instructive glances such as "Don't even think
about it" or "Do go on—I'm interested." Dogs are masters at reading these human expressions.

Since many of our Canine Assistants recipients cannot speak or
make significant hand signals, we take advantage of dogs' amazing attention to people's eyes, teaching thirty-two different behaviors
cued by eye movement only. For example, if we want a dog to
"down," we simply look at the dog's eyes and then at the floor.
Provided the dog has already been taught to lie down on verbal and
hand signal cues, he will follow our gaze and think, *What behavior do
I do involving the floor?* Most dogs are fairly quick to figure out what
the cue means and respond appropriately. Once they do, we reward

and praise them with such enthusiasm that they clearly understand they made the correct decision. We then apply the same principle to more complex behaviors, such as tugging open a door. Looking at a dog, then looking at the door the dog has previously been taught to tug open, eventually results in his tugging open the door with just a glance.

Most of our new recipients worry a great deal about their ability to manage a dog given the extent of their disabilities. Many of them cannot physically give the appropriate cues; many have difficulty remembering the appropriate cues. But those worries are unnecessary. My years at Canine Assistants have taught me that people and dogs, when bound together by loving trust, develop a beautiful, fluent language of their very own.

CHAPTER TEN

The Canine Character

Ben's warm honey-colored eyes seemed far too wise to belong to a fourteen-year-old boy. His mother, Clair, had eyes that were the same light brown as her son's, but unlike his, Clair's eyes were shuttered with unspeakable pain. She had asked me to visit them in Ben's hospital room at the Shepherd Center in Atlanta.

The Shepherd Center is an amazing place. In theory, it is a rehabilitation hospital for people who have suffered brain and spinal-cord injuries. In reality, it is a place where life starts over again for people who have been injured and for their families. Patients come from all over the world to Shepherd for treatment; Ben and Clair had come up from Florida. Visiting with our dogs allows patients a glimpse of how life can be lived in a wheelchair. Surprisingly, visiting Shepherd isn't depressing. The facility is all about moving forward; at Shepherd, failure is not an option.

Still, visits to Shepherd can be very intense, mostly because of the stories behind each injury. Ben's story was difficult to hear. Clair, a single mother, had just picked Ben up from school. On the drive home, he told his mother that a girl he was crazy about had invited him to a concert the following Saturday night. Ben was sky-high about the date—until his mom told him that she wouldn't let him go. She felt that the band they were going to see had a following that was too mature and much too wild for fourteen-year-olds. The two began to argue and, distracted by the quarrel, Clair ran a red light. A semitruck hit them broadside, crushing the passenger's side and sending the car spinning to a stop nearly a hundred yards down the road. Ben's spinal cord was severed. Clair and the truck driver were not hurt.

When we first met at Shepherd, Clair simply wanted Ben to spend some time with Nick. Both mother and son were dog lovers and had recently lost their twelve-year-old collie to cancer. Nick liked Ben and would happily spend time up on his bed, but he adored Clair. Nick had an unerring ability to identify the person in the room who needed him the most and to focus his affection on that individual. Clair was definitely that person. Her ex-husband hadn't been in contact with the family since a week after Ben's birth, her mother had died two years prior, and her father was in a nursing home with advanced Alzheimer's. With the exception of a brother she hadn't seen in many years, Clair was alone in the world with her badly injured child.

After Ben's release from Shepherd, I lost contact with the family for almost two years. One morning as I came into the office at Canine Assistants, I was pleasantly surprised to see a message in my box from Ben. The message stated specifically that I was to call him only between ten a.m. and two p.m., the time of the day when his mom would be at her part-time job. When the clock hit ten that morning, I called. An aide answered and put the phone on speaker mode so that I could talk with Ben. He assured me that he and his mom were getting along okay but that she was driving him insane. "She feels so guilty," Ben said, wheezing out the words laboriously through the ventilated air that kept him alive. "She won't leave me alone for one second. I can't take it anymore. I want to be left by myself every now and then. Can you talk to Mom for me?" I said I would try and promised to call back when his mom was home later that evening.

Under the premise of checking on them, I phoned Clair that night. After a few minutes of small talk, her voice suddenly became tight and serious. She feared that Ben's ventilator would shut off and that she would not be able to hear the alarm if she wasn't in his room. When the alarm sounded, she explained, a switch needed to be flipped quickly, resetting the machine so that Ben could breathe once again. She hadn't had a shower that lasted longer than about sixty seconds since Ben's accident.

"What if we could teach a dog to listen for the alarm and alert you if it goes off?" I asked. "Then you both could have a little freedom." Though initially skeptical, she grew to embrace the idea, and I put the wheels in motion.

Fortunately, our waiting list was not so long in those days. The wonderful people at Milk-Bone were willing to provide a sponsorship for Ben, and we were able to get him into a training camp just six months after our conversation. Once at our facility, a little golden female named Roxie fell in love with Ben. While Roxie knew all of her basic and advanced commands, we needed to customize her repertoire to include listening for and reacting to Ben's ventilator alarm. Roxie proved herself a quick and capable student. While her attention was squarely on Ben, she, like Nick, was eager to give Clair much-needed affection from time to time. When Ben and Clair headed back to Florida after camp, I felt good about the impact Roxie was going to have on their lives.

I would check in with the trio occasionally over the first few months, and hearing that things were working out well, I relaxed my concern for them. Over time, they moved to the back of my mind. Months later, when I received a call from Clair, I was startled and immediately apprehensive. Everything was okay, she explained, but she had an amazing story to tell me about Roxie.

Roxie had learned her job well and had run to alert Clair on two occasions when Ben's alarm sounded. That morning, the alarm had gone off and Ben watched as Roxie scampered out of the room in search of his mother. However, Clair wasn't in the house. She had gone down the driveway to retrieve the mail, a quick daily ritual. While she was at the box, their neighbor had come over and the two chatted for a few moments. Apparently, those were the very moments when Roxie was trying to find Clair. Before Ben lost consciousness, he saw Roxie run behind his chair. When Clair returned to the house, Roxie ran up, grabbed her sleeve, and pulled her back to Ben's room. Although the young man had passed out for a few moments, he was already beginning to regain his senses. When his breath returned completely, Ben was able to describe what had happened. The reset switch on the ventilator had been flipped. Clair was stunned by the possibility that Roxie had flipped the switch herself, but there was no other explanation. Since all of our dogs are taught the cue "switch" to facilitate the turning on of lights, Clair's story seemed plausible. Roxie was merely doing what she had seen Clair do.

Before her call to me, Clair had taken Roxie to the vet's office. She'd noticed that Roxie was limping and badly bleeding from around her nails on both front paws. There was blood on the back of Ben's chair and all over the floor of the house. Their veterinarian said it looked as if Roxie had clawed at something so hard that it rubbed her nails down into the quick, a part of a dog's nail that is extremely sensitive and apt to bleed profusely when damaged.

On the ride home, Clair and Ben speculated about what Roxie could have gotten into, thoroughly puzzled. After coming through the front door, Ben turned his wheelchair around to watch his mother and Roxie come into the house. That's when he noticed the marks. When Ben's alarm had sounded, Roxie needed to alert Clair. But she was outside, down at the street. In an effort to get to her, Roxie had been desperately scratching at the big wooden front door. The marks were bloody and deep. After seeing them, Clair collapsed to the floor, crying and hugging Roxie.

The marks were proof that Roxie was not only very clever but also caring enough to cause herself harm in a frantic effort to get help for the young man she loved. While we teach many things at Canine Assistants, the compassion displayed by our dogs is not a learned ability; it is purely an inherent trait.

The more I learned about the cognitive abilities, emotions, and personalities of dogs, the more I realized that something necessary to fully appreciate the true essence of dogs was missing. Yes, intelligence and emotion and personality all formed a wonderful circle, each attribute connected to the others as they jointly formed the whole. But there was something else, something both ethereal and all-powerful, that surrounded the species. It wasn't until I heard the story about Ben and Roxie that I realized what that missing piece was: character.

Just a few months after Roxie performed her heroic deed, I had several somewhat serious health issues of my own to contend with and had to spend six months in bed. With free time forced on me, I spent all day every day researching various dog-related subjects, specifically canine cognition and emotionality. What I learned, and the theories I developed from that information, led me to rewrite the Canine Assistants Recipient Teaching Manual. As I was trying to decide what information to include and how to categorize it, I encountered a dilemma. In dogs, there exist positive qualities, such as empathy and loyalty, that are interwoven within the categories of cognition, emotion, and personality, yet they cannot be strictly classified under one of those categories alone. In the manual, I decided to label these canine qualities "character," using the word to signify "a group of positive traits."

Character requires two unique and complex abilities: First, a dog must have theory of mind, an understanding of his own mental state and that of another. Next, character requires a conscious willingness to do what is in the best interest of another; though self-interest may also be served, it is not necessarily the motivating factor.

Theory of mind is the recognition that others have mental states, such as intentions and beliefs, and that those states are different from one's own. A recent study from Birkbeck College, University of London, supports the concept that dogs have theory of mind. It appears that dogs yawn when we yawn. In humans, the lack of susceptibility to contagious yawning has been linked to poor performance on theory-of-mind tests. Conversely, those humans who *were* susceptible to contagious yawning demonstrated empathy and other characteristics that some researchers believe allow for significantly better results on such tests. Dogs didn't merely perform well on the "yawn test"; they appreciably outscored the other study subjects—humans and chimpanzees. Dogs yawned in response to their owner's yawns 72 percent of the time, while people responded to the yawns of other people 45 to 60 percent of the time, and chimpanzees only 33 percent of the time.

The word "consciousness" is often used to mean "awake and aware of what is going on." However, for our purposes we need to assign a deeper, more philosophical meaning. Scientists have been trying for many years to come up with a standard definition of the word, but since they are bound by the exacting standards of science, a consensus has been difficult to achieve. I am not so bound, so in my book, consciousness is the awareness of and willful reaction to thoughts and feelings. It is the ability to think about and act on our thoughts and feelings. For example, fear is a subconscious response to sensory input, but bravery is a conscious response to fear.

Many scientists still refuse to acknowledge that dogs exercise conscious awareness. But there is more credible evidence that consciousness exists in dogs than evidence to the contrary. Perhaps they do not experience consciousness in the same manner as humans do, since it is unlikely that dogs spend an inordinate amount of time wondering about the origins of the universe. Yet, at the same time, it *is* likely that dogs *do* sit around and worry about us. Think about the awareness demonstrated by the service dog Roxie when she flipped the switch to reset Ben's ventilator. At Canine Assistants, Roxie was taught to respond when the alarm went off, but it was her own conscious assessment of the situation that led her to figure out what to do about it.

Theory of mind and consciousness are necessary components of the quality that forms the bedrock of canine character: empathy. Simply put, empathy is the ability to put oneself in another's position, to understand and to some degree experience their thoughts and feelings. Not surprisingly, there is much controversy among experts as to whether or not dogs are capable of empathy. I am personally convinced that dogs can empathize. Though complex, empathy appears to be a necessary skill for social animals who engage in co-operative efforts such as hunting and communal living. The need to feel what others are feeling seems paramount to coordinating efforts successfully. In animals like wolves and dogs, for whom group harmony is of great importance, empathy must exist.

Because of a brain injury as a young adult, Troy required that his wife, Judy, give him hard, sharp slaps on the back to help clear his lungs. The procedure wasn't pleasant, but it was necessary for his care. The first time Troy's service dog, Kay, witnessed the lung-clearing, she was horrified. Initially, Kay whined and barked. Then she attempted to paw Judy's hand away. When those efforts didn't work, Kay laid her head on Troy's back, prepared to absorb the next blow. Such tenderness is clear evidence to me of empathy.

Another positive trait possessed by dogs is the willingness to co-operate, usually in a manner that is immediately beneficial to others rather than to self. Cooperation is evidence of significant cognitive ability, but more than that, it is further evidence of character. Dogs can and do cooperate brilliantly with one another and with humans. They herd with us, hunt with us, work with us, and patrol with us. They guide us when our vision fails, pick up dropped items when we cannot, get help for us when we are unable to get it for ourselves, and do so much more that benefits us but is rarely of immediate benefit to them.

The desire to make others happy is an inherent trait of canines. Dogs seem to comfort those in need instinctively. When Nick and I would do school presentations together, he always chose a particular child to whom he would give the vast majority of his attention. After the presentation, a teacher or school official would invariably comment on Nick's choice of child: "It's almost as if he knew that Toby has cancer," and "How did that wonderful dog know how much Erin has been going through with her parents' divorce?" and even "How did your dog know that that boy's mother just died?" Nick's ability to discern emotional wounds was amazing, but I was always left speechless by his desire to heal those wounds. Nick wanted to make things better.

On the day my mom died, Kent's dog, Case, would not stop

clowning around. He grabbed the newspaper from the driveway and ran recklessly around the yard before putting the paper in my hands. He leaped, he rolled, he woofed, and generally played the role of the court jester. At the time we commented that Case, with his silliness in the face of tragedy, was a poor mourner. Upon reflection, I realized that Case was, in his own goofy way, trying desperately to lighten the emotional mood. He wanted us to feel better. Though he was always something of a clown, Case had never before, nor did he ever again, behave the way he did that day.

When I was a little girl, our neighbors the Hills had a remarkable border collie named Daphne. One Friday afternoon, Mr. Hill came home with a little terrier-mix dog that he had found in a gas-station parking lot. The dog was elderly and in very poor condition. Mrs. Hill tried to feed the stray some of Daphne's dog food. Though he looked longingly at the kibbles, he refused to eat. The Hill family was baffled, and the more they tried to feed the dog, the less responsive he became. Daphne, on the other hand, knew exactly what to do. She took kibble from her own bowl and chewed it into tiny pieces, holding it in her mouth for a few moments to moisten it. Then she spat the soft mush onto the floor in front of the stray. He gobbled it up. Daphne patiently chewed and softened all the food in her bowl until the old dog was fed. A visit to the vet the following morning confirmed what Daphne must have suspected: The dog had two abscessed teeth, one on either side of his mouth, making chewing difficult and terribly painful. Daphne had figured out what was wrong with the other dog and, incredibly, cared enough to prepare his food for him.

When Canine Assistants first started, we would occasionally take dogs to use in the program from owners who could no longer keep them. This practice was discontinued once we realized that many of the people who had donated the dogs suddenly decided that they wanted them back, after we had spent months working with them.

One wintry evening, before the flaw in the program became apparent, I agreed to meet a man at our facility to evaluate his female

Lab mix, whom he wanted to donate to us. We required owners to remain in their cars while we tested the dogs so that they weren't distracted or influenced by the presence of a loved one. Once the man handed me the dog's leash, he returned to his car. The dog and I were alone in the testing area except for three of our dogs-in-training, who were in crates finishing their evening meals. The man's dog was tense, so I dropped her leash and turned around to get some treats to feed her. As I turned back around, I was shocked to see that the dog had launched herself off the ground and was in midair, headed directly for my throat, her eyes blackened and her teeth bared. I had just enough time to throw my arm across my neck before she grabbed me. I would like to think that I have learned enough in the twenty years since this incident to know better than to turn my back on such a fearful dog. She was not inherently mean or vicious, she was simply terrified; fearing that I might hurt her, she struck out in defense of that prospect. Of course, I wasn't going to hurt her, but she had no way of knowing that.

That knowledge was of little use at the time. The sixty-pound dog was latched tightly on to my left arm as I held her up by the back of the neck with my right, hoping to prevent her from tearing downward on the part of me locked between her teeth. I was rapidly weakening and sank to my knees. The dog was about to do some serious damage, and since I was without help, I was beginning to wonder if I had gotten myself into a potentially life-threatening situation. In any case, I knew it wasn't good. Apparently, so did the three dogs in crates against the wall. I didn't realize it, but all three of them had gotten loose. The two black Lab males, Zulu and Alex, each grabbed one of the attacking dog's back legs and began to pull, as Lucy, the border collie, rushed toward the dog's face. As the male Labs got the dog to release me, Lucy placed herself between my attacker and me, preventing further assault. At last, my three dogs gained control of the situation and I was able to run for the other dog's owner.

Lucy and I both ended up having surgery that night. My arm was broken where the dog had bitten through the bone, and there were several long rips in the skin that needed stitches. Lucy required significant reconstructive work on her face.

Weeks later, I was crushed to hear that the owner had his dog put to sleep. Somewhere in her life, people had failed her so badly that she resorted to attacking first and asking questions later. As it turned out, the man had wanted to get rid of the dog because she was so aggressive. He did not seem to care what kind of companion his dog might have made for a child in a wheelchair. For my part, I was devastated to cause, however inadvertently, the death of another living being, even one who had hurt me badly.

It seems likely that my dogs knew I was in trouble that day, and I'm certain they responded as they did because they cared about me. While I may come across as sentimental in my assessment of the situation, to my mind, those dogs risked their lives to save me. Dogs, with their clear ancestral code of moral conduct, do not like other dogs who stray outside the bounds of appropriate behavior any more than people do.

I was quoted in Sharon Sakson's marvelous book *Paws & Effect* as saying: "The only indication of lack of intelligence in dogs I've ever seen is their willingness to forgive us for so much." As Sharon clearly captures, the statement was made tongue in cheek. It isn't stupidity on the part of a dog that keeps him returning to his owner even after poor treatment; it is a combination of absolute forgiveness and an innocent lack of awareness that others can possess less-than-sterling character. It is most unfortunate that dogs who lose their innocence, like the one who attacked me, end up getting themselves in terrible trouble.

Dogs are creatures of immense character, and people would do well to emulate their compassion, forgiveness, and caring when living and working with them. We have a clear responsibility, as their human leaders, to educate dogs as to our expectations and personal code of conduct; however, we have no right to do so through the use of fear or force. Dogs are too easily taught using more-compassionate methods. They have set a high standard in their interactions with humans, and it is our responsibility to uphold that standard.

CHAPTER ELEVEN

The Serious Business of Play

Several years ago I received an email entitled "Polar Bear Plays with Dog." I deleted it without even opening it. Later that afternoon Meghan, my assistant, asked if I'd seen the email and the remarkable photographs it contained. "No way," I replied. "I don't want to see a polar bear mauling a dog."

"The bear just plays with the dog," she said. "You need to see these amazing pictures." As usual, she was absolutely correct. As I looked at the photos of a polar bear, one of nature's great predators, playing happily with an Alaskan husky, I realized how truly transcendent play is.

Nature photographer Norbert Rosing took those incredible shots and an accompanying video. He was on the western coast of Canada's Hudson Bay, ostensibly to take sunset photos of a team of huskies belonging to a local dogsledder. As Rosing prepared his equipment, a polar bear ambled onto the scene and within a few moments was playing gently with the dogs. It is unlikely the bear had eaten anything for many months, as his hunting grounds were frozen, yet he never appeared aggressive or predatory. The bear returned to their campsite every evening for a week to play with the dogs. He disappeared only when the ice had melted enough for him to begin hunting for seals once again.

When Nick was about a year old, he and I first went to the beach together. We had been invited to a children's hospital in Jacksonville, Florida, and we took advantage of our proximity to one of my favorite places, the barrier islands of coastal Georgia, and extended our trip. We stayed overnight on St. Simons Island at a wonderful old Methodist retreat called Epworth By The Sea and hung out the next day on the beach.

As we prepared to head back to Atlanta in the early evening, I walked Nick to the edge of the woods near our lodge so that he could relieve himself before the six-hour journey home. Suddenly, Nick stopped and looked intently into the woods. In a flash, he bolted after something, pulling so quickly and hard that the leash was ripped from my hand. I had to go only about fifty feet before catching sight of him again. He was at a clearing, sniffing a young fawn. In a moment, the young deer bounded off through the woods with Nick in pursuit. I was afraid that he was going to hurt the fawn, but then Nick turned and ran the other way. Amazingly, the fawn reversed course too, chasing after Nick. For several minutes they turned and twisted and darted through the trees. The two of them, predator and prey, playing joyfully, until the small deer tired and Nick jogged back to me. While the interaction had been fascinating, its significance did not occur to me until several years later, after I saw the polar bear video. Play is so powerful as to render other concerns, such as the difference between species and their associated proclivities, irrelevant.

In my position at Canine Assistants, I have received many notes from recipients and their families describing how their dogs have brought laughter and play back into their world. I used to dismiss these kind messages as nice but of relatively little importance. After seeing the polar bear at play with his newly found dog friends and reading about other such interactions, I came to the realization that play is important—for us, for our dogs, and for our relationship.

Just what is play? It's hard to say. My attempts to break down the concept into a tidy definition tend to become ridiculously convoluted, a jumble of meaningless words. Try defining it yourself and you'll see what I mean. In an effort to come to terms with the meaning of play, I settled for listing its attributes.

Play must:

Be fun. For some people, gardening, running, or tennis is play; for others, building sand castles, sewing, or reading can be play. When play ceases to be fun it can no longer be considered play.

Lack immediate practical intent. We play simply because it is fun. If benefits are derived from so doing, they are secondary to the joy of play itself.

Employ behaviors out of practical context. Teaching a dog to fetch is practical for a hunter who needs his dog to retrieve game. Throwing a ball for your dog to chase is play that employs a practical behavior—in this case, retrieving—out of context.

Incorporate exaggerated movements and postures. Playing capture the flag is an exaggerated version of grabbing a resource, such as food, and running it to a safe place. Dogs that are "play-fighting" use much more exaggerated biting motions and body postures than those that would be involved in a genuine fight.

Not be undertaken with the intent to harm the other player(s). While bad things can happen during play, no one enters into true play wishing harm to his opponent or expecting to be harmed himself.

Be started by the player(s). Play is always self-initiated, even though one player can encourage another to begin playing.

Involve self-handicapping when participants are unevenly matched. Because the purpose of play is enjoyment, stronger players will often handicap themselves in order to keep from hurting weaker players. The numerical handicap utilized by golfers is an example of humans balancing the playing field. Nick could easily have harmed the fawn—or the polar bear the huskies—had he not self-handicapped.

At times include role reversal. Role reversals are not unique to human games. Just as there is turn-taking between offense and defense in many of our people games, there is offense and defense in most dog play. For example, dogs will take turns chasing each other.

Make participants less aware of time. When fully involved in play, we tend to forget about constraints like time and self-consciousness. Play pulls us into another, less rigorously defined dimension.

People and dogs are species that continue to play into adulthood. For many animals, play is used as a kind of training for the young but is discontinued after maturation. Predatory animals are more likely to play as adults than are prey animals, and highly social creatures are the most likely of all to play as adults. Those animals who play the most as adults are those that are the most neotenized. Think about how juvenile in action and behavior dogs are in comparison to wolves and how closely humans resemble juvenile chimpanzees, with our big eyes and our high, round foreheads. In both adult wolves and adult chimpanzees, behaviors are much more rigidly fixed: eat, sleep, breed, and stay safe, with much less chance of playful innovation. In adult dogs and humans, play constitutes a significant and essential part of our lives.

Few scientists have done research into play, but those who have, like biologist Marc Bekoff and neurobiologist Jaak Panksepp, speculate that play must be beneficial or it would not continue to occur. Most animals live a harsh existence—gathering food, staying safe, and procreating are of paramount importance—so for some animals to expend valuable energy playing certainly gives credence to the practical concept that play is of biological benefit to those that do it.

But play can also be dangerous. It calls attention to individuals by generating noise; it absorbs the attention of participants, making them vulnerable to predators; and the activities themselves can cause accidental injury. Yet, in spite of the inherent dangers, certain animals continue to play, providing further support for the argument that play has adaptive value. After all, two of the most successful creatures on the planet today, people and dogs, are among nature's greatest players.

There are numerous ways in which play can be considered bio-logically beneficial. Play helps with gross- and fine-motor-skills de-velopment. Catching a ball develops hand and eye coordination. Sewing, woodworking, and even stacking building blocks tunes fine-motor skills. For animals, retrieving works eye and mouth co-ordination in addition to stalking skills. Play also allows for explo-ration of places and things in one's environment, while sharpening the ability to rapidly assess and compensate for the movement pat-terns of others. It facilitates social bonds, supports efforts of individ-uals to better understand one another, and can even ascertain social status among individuals. Play makes us happier and healthier, pro-viding mental relaxation and increasing our physical energy. Whether for one or all of these reasons, playfulness clearly provides an adaptive advantage for some species.

The desire and ability to play is apparently genetically coded into us. Children and puppies are born with the ability to play. It is not something that must be taught; it is hardwired into both species. Neurobiologist Panksepp explains, "That play is a primary emo-tional function of the mammalian brain was not recognized until re-cently, but now the existence of such brain systems is a certainty."

Hunger, safety, and social attachment seem to be more impor-tant than play. If an animal is hungry, stressed, or lonely, he is unlikely to play. But, given a full belly, a safe environment, and maybe a friend or two, he becomes nearly impossible to stop from playing. Individuals who are denied the opportunity to play with others will play by themselves. It isn't at all uncommon to see a dog alone in a yard, playing chase by himself. I once watched a dalmatian play an adapted version of hide-and-seek with a sprinkler.

Play can occur individually or it can be social in nature, involv-ing more than one. Since the more social the species, the more likely they are to play, it is no surprise that dogs prefer to play with others. In a litter of puppies, social play begins at around three to four weeks of age. Dogs prefer playing one on one in what is called a dyad. Often, when a third dog comes in, things get dicey and fights are more likely to break out. However, that does not mean that three dogs cannot play together. While I have watched groups of three play well together every day at Canine Assistants, things seem to run more smoothly in pair play. And, though we see no gender preference when puppies are young, as they grow older, males seem to pair with other males and females with other females when it's time to play.

Every day I stand at my office window and watch the dogs as they go out for recess. Our dogs live in groups, and it is with their kennelmates that they play. The movements executed are equal parts fascinating and comedic. They bow, they spin, they chase, they flip, and they bite. From countless hours spent watching both our dogs and other dogs play, I have realized that every individual has his own primary style. While styles can be affected by various factors and change depending on the situation and the company, there is definitely an overall play personality to each dog.

No matter what the style, social play is critical for dogs. It teaches them to play by the rules. It helps give participants a clear idea of what is right and wrong, what works and what does not work. It also teaches trust, cooperation, negotiation skills, and even forgiveness. In social animals, play is the basis for being able to function as part of a group, and animals that live in groups must be able to work for their mutual survival. For us, watching dogs at play allows a look at their personalities in action and a chance to better understand how they work.

One day I took a young female golden, Lulu, home to help refine her retrieving skills. However, before we settled in to work, I wanted her to have some relaxing playtime in my big fenced-in yard. Though Nick went out too, as a playmate for Lulu, he totally ignored the young female dog, choosing instead to wander casually about the yard and warm himself in the sun. But Lulu was full of energy and anxious to play. She did everything she could to entice Nick into her games. When he was looking at her, she used a play bow, lowering her front legs and raising her bottom, to invite him to join her. When Nick was not looking at her but wasn't engaged in anything else, Lulu gave a little yip in an effort to gain his attention.

PLAY PERSONALITY	PRIMARY STYLE
The Streaker	The Streaker is pure speed, and he loves to show it. Given his preference, he likes to play "catch me if you can." At Canine Assistants, we turn the tables on the Streaker by chasing him for a moment, then reversing direction and encouraging him to chase us. This is an excellent way to keep his attention focused on us.
The Repeater	This dog is tireless. He is the one who wants his partner to chase him again. In play with people, his lament is "Throw it again. Again. Again. Again." The Repeater may be a little obsessive-compulsive. We save our sanity when working with a Repeater by being sure that each throw of his favorite toy involves lots of either physical or mental exercise. We often use a tennis racket or golf club to get as much distance on each throw as possible, or we "hide" the toy in a low tree branch or under a couch so he has to think about how to retrieve it.
The Pouncer	The Pouncer plays a game of his own devising where he scores points for bouncing himself off the body of his playmate. He is a master of the play bow, as he means no harm by his game. When we play with the Pouncer, we are very careful to keep him from running into us, as many a knee has been blown out this way. We prefer teaching the Pouncer to retrieve, so we can redirect his energies into a safer game.
The Breeder	As you can imagine, the Breeder thinks play is just good practice for mating day. Breeders often have a tough time finding a partner, but once they do, they are more than willing to alternate positions. We redirect the Breeder into other, more socially appropriate games, like hide-and-seek, in order to avoid awkward conversations with visiting children.

PLAY PERSONALITY	PRIMARY STYLE
The Tooth Flasher	The Tooth Flasher loves nothing better than a ferocious-looking game of toothy-tooth, recognizable by open-mouth tooth-to-tooth contact. For the Tooth Flasher, teeth wrestling rules. The Tooth Flasher is likely to be a dog who loves retrieving and other activities involving the mouth. We are sure the Tooth Flasher always has appropriate chew toys so our shoes don't become increasingly ventilated.
The Talker	She barks, she growls, she yelps. The Talker says it all. She invites and punctuates her play vocally. This is an expressive, communicative dog whose vocal style can easily be misunderstood—i.e., someone may mistake her playful growls for a genuine threat. Talkers are always fun for us to watch play and are great at two-way communication.
The Monitor	Play for the Monitor is all about keeping others playing by the rules. Monitors can be seen wherever dogs gather, enforcing the rules of polite play. At Canine Assistants, our Monitors keep the other dogs in line, thus making our lives much easier. As confident as they appear, however, Monitors need structure in order to feel safe, so we try to keep our daily routines stable.

When he was actively involved with something else, like sniffing the rosebushes, Lulu would let out a big, happy bark as if to say, "The fun is over here with me." She demonstrated incredible cleverness in her attempts to engage Nick, tailoring her level of exertion according to his degree of inattention. This is a clear indicator of theory of mind in dogs. Lulu knew that Nick was a separate being from her, with thoughts and desires of his own, and that she must connect with him if she hoped to have a play partner. Finally, after many minutes and multiple overtures, Lulu captured Nick's attention, and he spent the next thirty minutes chasing and being chased, grabbing and tugging, and pouncing and bouncing with her.

Dogs are clever at the business of playing. While bows are often an invitation to play—as Lulu did with Nick—they can also be used as a form of metacommunication. Metacommunication explains how to interpret impending actions or information. For example, when a play bow is used prior to one dog pouncing on another, the bow means, "My pounce is not intended as aggression; it's purely play"—an action straight from the Pouncer's playbook.

Bows are also used by dogs to call a brief time-out during interactions, when excitement levels begin to tip play into aggression. Dogs seem to realize instinctively that breaks in the action are important for keeping things friendly. They even self-handicap when playing with other dogs who are not as big or as strong as they are. In addition, role reversals are common, with one dog being the chaser first and then assuming the role of the chased. Watching healthy play in dogs is like watching a ballet—thrilling yet effortlessly fluid.

Play between humans and dogs provides all the benefits of conspecific dog-on-dog play, increasing trust and confidence between partners. Ever since I brought Nick home as a puppy, I have tried to spend at least a few minutes every day engaged in play with each of my dogs, throwing the tennis ball or wrestling and rolling around with them. While I am careful to keep each dog from becoming overly aroused—which increases accidental-bite potential—I am never concerned about who wins. There is a commonly held belief, put forward by many of today's dog trainers, that people should always "win" when playing with their dogs or run the risk of losing their dog's respect. This is nonsense. Dogs know that play is just that—play, complete with numerous role reversals. The idea of winning or losing respect during play seems much more of a people problem than anything that might occur to a dog. Dogs are virtual play experts and appear to clearly understand the differences between recreation and serious business.

My favorite game to play with my own dogs and with dogs-in-training at Canine Assistants is hide-and-seek. Hide-and-seek keeps your dog's attention focused on you. You can play inside or in a safely fenced area. Just duck behind a piece of furniture or a doorway and see how long it takes your dog to come looking for you. My son and I like to teach our dogs to stay until we get into our hiding places and then we ask them to "seek." A silly child's game provides an excellent teaching exercise and an entertaining playtime.

One of the most commonly heard expressions in the world of dog training is "A tired dog is a good dog." I completely agree with this notion. Dogs who don't get enough exercise often exhibit unacceptable behaviors such as chewing on the curtains or barking incessantly. Dogs who get adequate exercise are more likely to conform willingly to household rules.

There is a strong link in dogs, as in people, between good mental health and exercise. Dogs who exercise are far less likely to exhibit anxiety-related behaviors. As a matter of fact, when dogs play, they often laugh. Dr. Patricia Simonet, an ethologist at Sierra Nevada College in Lake Tahoe, Nevada, researched the vocalizations of playing dogs and found what can best be described as laughter. The laughter of a dog sounds like panting, with a particular "hhuh hhah hhuh hhah" pattern. Dr. Simonet noted that people can recreate these breathy exhalations, to the delight of their dogs. Not only do I use the doggy laugh sound to encourage dogs to play with me, I also use it to help calm dogs when they are feeling anxious. Try it with your dog. You will know you've gotten the sound right when your dog either runs to you or gives you his undivided attention. Dr. Stanley Coren, in a recent edition of *Psychology Today,* suggests that you round your lips slightly on the "hhuhs" and smile on the "hhahs." Remember, the sound is produced by your audible breathing pattern, not by actual speech.

Physical exercise isn't all a dog needs, however. Mental exercise can be every bit as important, and tiring, for dogs. We keep puzzle-type toys on hand for our dogs-in-training, to supplement physical exercise when outdoor exercise isn't possible. We also keep our dogs mentally exercised by teaching them new behaviors.

At Canine Assistants, the most successful long-term partnerships between recipients and assistance dogs are those that are the most playful. When I consider what makes a team function well, playfulness tops the list. It allows the pair to develop trust and understanding while the partners get "in synch." It permits each partner to produce feelings of joy in the other, reinforcing the pleasurable feelings derived from being together. Play is powerful. These days, I spend less time encouraging our recipients to work with their dogs and more time encouraging them to play with their dogs. Best of all, through play, dogs have the continuing opportunity for lifelong learning.

CHAPTER TWELVE

Choice Teaching

We wanted to see what Alice, a young golden retriever, would do if her teacher, Liza, fell down and asked Alice to go get help, a behavior the dog did not yet know. Liza threw herself convincingly on the floor and began imploring Alice, "Go get help." Three of us had stationed ourselves around the room, ready to spring into action should Alice come to us for help. She looked at Liza with great concern and lifted the paw of appeasement, as if to say, "I am really trying here, but I'm not sure what to do." She then looked hard at the three of us. Finally, her face lit up and she dashed to the cabinet on a nearby wall, pulled open one of the doors, and stuck her head inside. It was not clear what she had retrieved until she dropped it right in front of Liza's face. It was a bag of Milk-Bone treats, Alice's favorite. She must have felt that the three of us were likely to be useless, but good food is always helpful.

I love watching dogs process situations and figure out what they feel is the best course of action. It's like watching a child go through the same procedure. Though the response the dogs give may not necessarily be what we're looking for, it always makes a beautiful, uncomplicated kind of sense when viewed from the dogs' perspective. Alice knew Liza needed something, so she gave her what she would have most liked to receive: Milk-Bones. This shows us a great deal about both the cognitive abilities and limitations of our dogs.

Alice's behavior also illustrates another trait common among dogs. While she didn't quite understand Liza's request, she was trying to make her happy. Dogs don't always know what we want them to do, but they are generally willing to try to figure it out.

Ralph, an elderly cocker spaniel, loved to visit the house across the street to see what treats might be available inside. Miss Sadie, the old woman who lived in the house, baked a fresh batch of peanut butter cookies every Friday and handed them out to Ralph whenever he came to call. Jan, his owner, allowed him to cross the usually quiet street by himself, because he seemed to take great care to look in both directions. Ralph could still see well, though he could no longer hear at all. One day he made his way across the street and had what was reported by Miss Sadie to be a "lovely visit." As a matter of fact, Ralph was gone so long that Jan got worried and came outside to look for him. Jan spotted Ralph starting to cross the road a split second before she heard the horn and saw the speeding car. Knowing Ralph couldn't hear the horn, Jan frantically gestured to Ralph to "drop." This was a command at which he had excelled as a younger dog but hadn't done for many years. Seeing the gesture, Ralph dropped in place just off the curb, where the car easily missed him. This near-disaster proved both the value of training and the wisdom of a leash. Ralph's owner congratulated herself on her training efforts and henceforth walked him over for his cookies—firmly secured to a lead.

Life with a dog is far better if you *both* know some behaviors on cue. My golden retriever Nan has taught me to let her out when she approaches holding one of my shoes. This is the cue she uses to tell me she has a bathroom emergency. I am well trained.

Dogs also need to know behaviors on cue. These behaviors can then be used to help them understand a more general code of appropriate conduct. For example, teaching your dog the behaviors "off," "sit," and "shake" will allow you to make it clear that jumping up on people is not your preferred method of greeting. Teaching your dog also helps strengthen communication between the two of you while reinforcing your role as caretaker. I prefer the word "cue" to the word "command"—I am not the commanding type. But I realize that is merely semantics.

In order to teach dogs, we must understand how they learn. You may notice that I use the word "teach" rather than "train." Training is part of teaching, but only a small part. Training connotes reinforcing a physical skill, while teaching means helping someone grasp a concept. I can *train* a dog to do a simple physical task, such as picking up a wooden dumbbell used for retrieval training when it's dropped directly in front of him. But if I want him to pick up any item dropped—even if the item rolls under the couch—and return it to my hand, then I must *teach* him the concept of retrieval.

This approach allows dogs to think things through, rather than classically conditioning them to respond automatically to certain stimuli, as Pavlov's dogs did with the bell. In considering what I knew about dogs—their ability to think, their intense emotionality, their genetic heritage, their love of play, their desire to please, and all the rest—I realized they are capable of more than a simple rote response to stimuli: Dogs can learn. At Canine Assistants, when we teach our dogs to sit, we never push down on their rear ends or pull up on their collars. Those actions stimulate a reflexive response and eliminate the need for the dogs to process the request and figure it out for themselves.

All learning takes place through some form of association, whether the response generated is the result of deliberation or reflex. Our dogs learn to associate words or physical cues with behaviors we would like them to do or to stop doing. They must determine the meaning of the given direction through thought. For example, dogs learn to associate the word "sit" or a scooping gesture of the hand with putting their haunches on the ground.

Operant conditioning, as defined by B. F. Skinner, is the most commonly used technique in teaching associations and the most reliable method to ensure performance of desired behaviors. Operant conditioning is a learning-and-teaching theory based generally on Thorndike's Law of Effect, which states in essence that behaviors that are reinforced will become more likely to occur and behaviors that are not reinforced will become less likely to occur. Teaching with operant conditioning relies on the use of reinforcement and punishment. Reinforcement is anything that makes the behavior more likely to occur. It can be positive, meaning the addition of something such as a treat, or negative, meaning the removal of something unpleasant such as the tension on a choke collar. Punishment is anything that makes the behavior less likely to occur. As with reinforcement, punishment can be positive, meaning something is added such as a leash correction, or negative, meaning something is removed such as the possibility of receiving a treat.

Operant conditioning is often described using a quadrant:

POSITIVE REINFORCEMENT Giving a treat	POSITIVE PUNISHMENT Leash correction
NEGATIVE REINFORCEMENT Relaxing tension of a choke collar	NEGATIVE PUNISHMENT Removing the possibility of receiving a treat

There are many different teaching methodologies that apply the principles of operant reinforcement. When I am working at Canine Assistants or making a presentation elsewhere, I am often asked if teaching methods are not merely a matter of personal preference. My answer is always the same: Absolutely not. *Good methods rely on positive reinforcement and negative punishment.* Conversely, the techniques that employ negative reinforcement and positive punishment are at a minimum unpleasant and on the other end of the spectrum blatantly cruel. If you've used one of the harsh teaching models that I oppose, you are not alone. I, too, have used each method discussed in this chapter. I trained with them believing, at the time, that they were appropriate. Thanks to Nick and the many dogs I have worked with over the years, my mind has changed about the proper way to handle dogs.

The recent popular trend in dog training that follows the alpha model causes me grave concern. The alpha model is based on a flawed interpretation of how an alpha wolf acts and is unnecessary and unpleasant for the dog.

Under the alpha model, dog owners assume the role of "pack leader." Owners are taught to be dominant over their dogs. "Dominant" is not a pleasant word. To me, it brings forth an image of someone's neck being pinned to the floor by the thick-heeled black leather boot of some unseen individual. As my husband, Kent, once said, "If you are going to put your foot on someone's neck, you better be prepared to leave it there forever." While I realize that physical abuse is not what trainers using this model are trying to promote, it unfortunately grants permission to those who want to manhandle their dogs, for whatever reason. Detailed instructions are given on the appropriate times to physically dominate the dog by forcing him to submit, using what is known as the alpha roll. This procedure requires the person to flip the dog onto his back and put a hand across the dog's throat in an aggressive display of dominance; supposedly this emulates how an alpha wolf behaves. This is a seriously flawed concept.

Dogs are not wolves, and, even if they were, this model is based on an erroneous interpretation of how alpha wolves behave. As noted earlier, alphas are simply the wolves who can do as they please and are usually the biological parents of the other pack members. They are among the least likely pack members ever to be physically aggressive. Alpha wolves do not have to be aggressive—they are numero uno, the pack leaders, and everyone, including the alpha, recognizes it. Displays of "dominance" such as the alpha roll would be far more likely to undermine the authority of a true alpha than to advance it; genuine leaders do not have to behave in such a manner. Can you imagine the President of the United States choking someone for sitting in his chair in the Oval Office? This dominance model creates a teaching methodology that is totally inappropriate. Don't undermine your own authority with your dog by flaunting it inappropriately. Good leaders are calm, cool, and confident.

The whole idea of our dogs desiring to dominate us is vastly overblown. It's ironic that the very same people who believe dogs are basically unintelligent, unemotional robots are often the ones who caution against allowing our dogs to dominate us. If you sincerely believe that your dog is making a coordinated effort to dominate you, then you must also credit him with cognitive abilities far beyond what research indicates exist in dogs.

In a recent DVD about canine body language, a female trainer was evaluating dogs in shelters. She referred to all the animals who jumped up as "height seeking" and pointed out the dominant "height seekers" in the various shelters. One young, energetic Lab kept jumping up on the woman and, at one point, the dog's muzzle connected sharply with her nose. The trainer claimed that this was a "muzzle punch," a move sometimes made by "height seekers." While doing the evaluation, the woman noted her feelings. "I hate this dog," she announced. It showed. It was very apparent to me *and* undoubtedly to the young Lab that this woman was hostile to the dog.

The dog continued to jump up, not in an effort to somehow dominate the woman through "height seeking" and "muzzle punches" but in an attempt to make contact with her. It was not a prizefight; it was an evaluation at a shelter of an abandoned young Lab who was clearly desperate for attention. At one point in the segment, the trainer pointed out that the dog was employing calming signals, such as lip licking or yawning—a sign directly opposed to her supposed domination attempts. Yet the woman still failed to understand that the dog was not trying to be obnoxious.

Think about the most logical reason for the dog's actions. If another human had popped this woman in the nose or pushed her down and stood over her, it would have been rude. But it is highly unlikely the dog meant to be rude. Why would an attention-starved shelter dog abuse a person trying to give her attention? It makes a great deal more sense that the dog was simply trying to encourage the woman's attention. It is true that height is power to dogs, as it is to humans, but the dog was merely attempting to reach the woman's face in order to give what the dog felt was an appropriate greeting; she was not trying to stand above the woman in some macho effort to dominate her. The woman withheld her affection, making the dog even more frantic to appease her, while the simple solution would have been to kneel, allowing the dog to greet her. In the face of this woman's disdain, the unfortunate dog was using calming signals, to calm herself and to relax the woman in the hope that the two could connect. It is heartbreaking to see how often dogs are the victims of such grievous misconceptions.

A school for working dogs (not my own) decided to experiment with the use of electronic collars as a training tool for their dogs. These "e-collars," as they are euphemistically dubbed, are sophisticated versions of the old-fashioned shock collar. When triggered, as a punishment for a dog failing to comply with a command, they administer anywhere from a very mild zap, which proponents claim to be a mere "tap on the shoulder," to a walloping shock. As soon as word reached the program's supporters that these collars were being used, many were outraged. So the program decided to hold a demonstration to prove that the collars were both mild and extremely effective. On the day of the event, a large crowd had gathered in the main building at the facility. A trainer led out a young dog and gave the cue to sit. When the dog failed to do as directed, the trainer administered the mildest possible shock, whereupon the dog yelped, peed all over himself, and promptly ran away. E-collars are indeed effective—but effective at what exactly?

Proponents of the e-collar are offended by the term "shock collar." But no amount of name beautification or deception can change the reality. While today's shock collars are more advanced than older versions, with more and milder settings, the end result is still the same: They shock. This method of training and managing dogs is cruel—period. While it may in fact produce results, the costs are far too high. The lower settings on these collars are mild, but as my veterinarian husband once said, "Chinese water torture doesn't hurt, but it still makes you crazy." This is a lazy and disgusting way to treat dogs. It is difficult to believe that trainers still use these collars at all, much less that they are increasing in popularity.

If, as many proponents declare, the collar causes no pain or lasting ill effects, then why aren't we using them on our toddlers? Think how fast we could toilet-train our children with a shock collar. Of course, that notion is absurd. It is obviously true that dogs are not children, but they are thinking, feeling beings, as helplessly dependent on us as toddlers are. Some trainers claim that the shock collar is acceptable because in certain cases it saves the dog's life. When are those times? When a dog jumps the fence? Build a taller fence, or walk him on a leash. When a dog bolts out an open door? Teach him to wait, or put him in another room before you open the door. When a dog chases the cat? House them in different rooms while you teach the dog to do something else, like bring you a ball, every time he sees the cat run. Shock collars are the tools of trainers not willing or able to use other, more humane methods. Make no mistake about it: I place the blame for e-collars squarely on the shoulders of "professional" dog trainers.

At the request of a friend who trained her dog using an e-collar, I attended, without a dog, a training class where e-collars were not only recommended, they were required. This was the initial class in a new session, and there were many questions about the shock collars, as it was the first time most of the attendees had used one. The instructor was delighted to don the collar and shock himself to demonstrate how little pain the collar would cause on the lowest setting. But the amount of pain the collar generates should not even be a question. Collars need not cause any pain at all. And, remember, there is an enormous difference between the lowest setting and the highest. The instructor continually promised these loving dog owners that the collars would cause their dogs and their relationship with their dogs no harm. He lied and they believed him. After all, you go to a professional expecting sound advice on matters beyond your personal expertise. Trainers who advocate these collars either distort the truth or do not realize the ramifications. Hardly professional either way.

E-collars are, by definition, damaging to dogs. If the collars did not elicit fear in dogs, making them anxious about receiving a shock, they would not be effective at causing or inhibiting behavior. Fear is physically and mentally harmful. Long-term or repetitive exposure to fear causes distress. Distress causes damage to an individual's health and potential longevity through the elevation of cortisol and other stress-related hormones. Distress also reduces an individual's capacity for learning, performance, and affection.

The instructor whose class I audited also proclaimed, "Your dog will have no idea that you are the one causing the shock. He will think his action caused it." That is not true in the least. A study conducted in 2003 at Utrecht University in the Netherlands was used as part of a movement to ban the use of e-collars, as has been done in Wales. The study showed that dogs' body postures were consistently an inch closer to the ground whenever they saw the people who controlled their e-collar, whether or not the dog was wearing the collar at the time. For a dog, the lowering of the body toward the ground, also known as cowering, is an act of submission.

In addition, dogs may not be mentally capable of determining every possible behavior, or lack thereof, that might result in their receiving a shock when these collars are used for generalized training. They have a better chance to control the shock when the collars are used only to prevent a particular behavior, such as barking. But, as we've already seen, preventing a behavior can be done only when there is an understanding of what is causing the behavior in the first place. If you put an e-collar on a dog who is barking because of separation anxiety, he may stop barking and instead start having diarrhea all over the house.

Dogs have a more reasonable chance to figure out how to avoid the shock from electronic, or invisible, fences, though this is not the easiest and most effective form of barrier to use with dogs. A dog may take the shock given by the buried fence in order to reach something on the other side. And, once out, it is highly unlikely he will be willing to get shocked again to go back into the yard. With more-sensitive dogs, these fences can cause great and lasting anxiety issues, such as being unwilling to go into the yard at all. One St. Bernard I know has not taken a single step into his two-acre back-yard since his family installed underground fencing that caused him to be shocked to recognize the boundary. When they realized the issue, his family immediately dug up the system and installed a wooden fence, but the dog still won't go out that way. They have to walk him on a leash in the front yard and take him to a local park to play.

Also, while an invisible fence means the dog cannot go out of his yard without receiving a shock, it allows other dogs to get into his yard without consequence. This opens up a host of problems, not the least of which is that the dog may feel uncomfortable or insecure in his own yard. Finally, things can go wrong mechanically with these electronic fences. I have picked up numerous dogs who have run away after a storm knocked out their electronic fencing.

The reason so many people have chosen to use training methods that induce fear in dogs stems, in large part, from the fact that this is the way many "professionals" are currently instructing. In addition, my husband believes that people like to use dominating methods because they are effective rapidly and because it may seem liberating to be forceful enough to control another living being. There is, of course, an alternative. If positive reinforcement is used exclusively, not only is proper behavior taught but people can also feel good about doing what is in the best interest of their dogs. The true professionals have concluded that dogs are far less likely to have problems when taught using only positive reinforcement. Clearly, it's best for our dogs, and best for us.

For several years, we had been using a basic form of positive re-inforcement exclusively at Canine Assistants, and it was fairly effective. We didn't use punishment or correction, but neither did we want to let the dogs get away with not doing as we asked. Rather, we continued to repeat the cue until the dogs did what we asked or some approximation thereof. The problem we kept running into was that many of the dogs would go through a stage where they would become resistant to doing as asked. It was as if the dogs decided to "just say no" to any requested behaviors, looking away and tuning out their trainer.

It was my son, Chase, who helped me figure out what was happening. I was explaining to him how tough school had been for me as a child. I felt trapped there, and I spent most of my mornings trying to figure out how to skip school. So my mother, in her seemingly infinite wisdom, unlatched the trap. She sent me to school each day with a signed, but not dated, permission slip for early dismissal and a promise to come and get me if I ever felt like I had to leave. The first day I went off with that note tucked into my pocket, I fell in love with everything about school. In the eight years I carried the note, I never once used it. "I understand," Chase said. "You just needed to know you had a choice. I think everybody likes to have a choice."

I replayed what Chase said in my mind over and over that night. We weren't really giving our dogs a choice or even the illusion of choice in their training. We were, in essence, making them do as we asked but doing so in a nice way. Maybe the lack of choice was the missing component in our methodology. I thought of all I had learned about how dogs perceive and process things, about their abilities and limitations. I worked through the night, rewriting our teaching guidelines to give the dogs *choice*. For example, instead of teaching the puppies to walk calmly on our left side while on leash, I suggested trying it in a small, safely fenced area with the puppies off leash. When the pups would walk where we wanted them, we would give them little treats and great praise. When the puppies chose to run around, we'd do nothing to stop them; we simply wouldn't reward them for it. When the puppies settled in to walking calmly beside us, then we would slip on a leash and collar.

In the morning, I had our trainers try the new approach. It took less than an hour before they excitedly called me to watch their dogs. The dogs who had become resistant to doing such basic behaviors as "sit" were eagerly doing everything their trainers asked them to do. Dogs who had been unwilling to get into their kennel were now enthusiastically doing so. The difference? The trainers were cueing the dogs and offering them great reward if they did as asked, then the trainers were quiet and allowing the dogs to figure it out for themselves. Little by little, each dog decided that it was in his best interest to do as asked. Once the dog decided to perform a behavior, such as "kennel," of his own volition, the next time he was asked for that behavior he did it quickly and willingly. Thanks to my insightful young son, I finally understood what had been missing: choice.

At Canine Assistants, we teach our dogs using a method that I've named Choice Teaching. This method was developed over time as my understanding and appreciation of dogs and their capabilities grew. There are other types of teaching methods that use positive reinforcement exclusively, such as Ian Dunbar's lure-and-reward training and Karen Pryor's clicker training, that are also fair and effective.

In Choice Teaching, at no time (except in genuine emergencies) are dogs forced to do anything. Having a choice means that dogs are given the opportunity to think through what is being asked of them. Allowing dogs a choice prevents situations from developing that might lead to forceful responses. We have a saying around here: "Force works once and only once, so use finesse instead." I have an excellent illustration of this principle. At Canine Assistants, we have noticed that there comes a time for many of our teenage pups when they no longer want to jump into the back of SUVs. This seems to be in response to a combination of reasons, such as an enhanced awareness of surroundings, changes in visual perception due to increased height, and a lack of coordination during this growth period. Once, and only once, a volunteer pulled one of our dogs into the back of her vehicle by the leash. The dog got into the car because she simply had no other choice; it was forced on her. The following day, the dog would not step into the parking lot at all, grounding herself as she got close, and for two days after that, she refused to leave her kennel. Force can cause a post-traumatic stress–like reaction, hindering rather than helping educational efforts. For that reason, force is prohibited at Canine Assistants.

On the other hand, choice, or the perception thereof, creates a dog who willingly does what is asked of him, because he thinks it is his own idea. If one of our dogs doesn't want to go in to his crate, we will offer him a treat to do so. And, no, that will not make him refuse to go in without a treat. It will only make him view his crate in a positive light and therefore be more willing to go in the next time he is asked. Also, we are extremely patient with a dog as he decides whether it is worth going in the crate. The longest I have ever had to wait is seventeen minutes, but I would have waited as long as it took. Once a dog has decided of his own accord, the next time will be far quicker.

Choice-taught dogs aren't always as prompt to comply with requests as are dogs trained in other ways, but they are able to do extraordinary things—such as figure out how to flip the reset switch on a young man's ventilator.

Initially, our dogs are taught the meaning of cues through the use of lures. Lures are anything, such as treats or toys, that dogs will follow as they are moved. They serve as positive reinforcement because they are given to the dog if he does the requested behavior. Since the dog gets the treat only when he does as asked, lures also serve as negative punishment in the event that the dog does not comply. (For a list of the behaviors we teach and the lures and cues for each, see Appendix A.) For completing the task, the lure—usually a Milk-Bone treat or a lick of peanut butter—becomes the reward. Ultimately, the reward goes from being extrinsic, or externally provided to being largely intrinsic, or internally provided. The performance of the requested behavior becomes so strongly associated with warm feelings that merely doing the behavior is a satisfactory recompense (though we do still use extrinsic reinforcement on a random basis).

When I was a little girl, we lived in a house that was surrounded by huge pine trees, as are most homes in Georgia. My mother hated having pinecones in the yard, because she enjoyed going barefoot and the cones were hard and sharp. Mom used to pay me to pick up the pinecones, which made her really happy. So the payment and her happiness were a double dose of extrinsic reward for me. I haven't been paid to pick up pinecones in thirty years, but to this day I love picking them up. It gives me a warm, comfortable feeling. I am now intrinsically motivated to pick up pinecones. Ah, if only Mom had paid me to clean the house . . .

Since dogs do not crave money, at Canine Assistants we use food, which provides a critical component of our education methodology. Food is the fastest, most powerful method of capturing and holding a dog's attention. It is the initial motivator used when teaching any new behavior. Edible treats allow benevolent leadership to be reinforced while rewarding the dog's behavior. Food can also serve as encouragement toward good performance in the future. While some people believe that their dogs are not motivated by food, dogs who do not like such rewards are extremely rare. It is more likely that the dog is simply too nervous to eat. In fact, at Canine Assistants, we use a dog's willingness to accept treats as a gauge of his comfort level.

In order to keep our dogs from becoming too dependent on treats, we use them on a random, sporadic basis. This may sound counterintuitive, but it works. The experts in Las Vegas and Atlantic City realized long ago that people are most likely to continue gambling if they have a 20 percent—no better and no worse—chance of winning, and this has proven true for dogs as well. When you combine the good feelings from intrinsic reinforcement with the possibility that a treat might be forthcoming, you have created the perfect storm for behavior performance.

It is the Choice Teaching instructor's responsibility to help the dog decide that it is in his best interest to do as asked, without making him fear retribution. Since dogs are smart enough to want to please those upon whom they depend, their human's happiness is an enormous incentive. A majority of the time, the dog will do as cued, but if not, there are three basic reasons why:

- THE DOG DOES NOT UNDERSTAND THE REQUEST. It may take a dog several moments to figure out what is wanted, even when a lure is used. Dogs must be allowed ample time to decode the words.

- THE DOG'S MOTIVATION TO COMPLY IS NOT AS COMPELLING AS HIS MOTIVATION TO REFUSE. Dogs do what is in their best interest, as we all do. A dog simply must be convinced that it is in his best interest to do as asked.

- THE DOG IS NOT CAPABLE OR DOES NOT FEEL CAPABLE OF PERFORMING THE REQUESTED BEHAVIOR. The dog may feel too vulnerable to perform certain behaviors, especially when around other dogs. Or perhaps he feels unable to please his owner, making him less likely to try. Success begets self-confidence, which begets success.

One evening I sat on the floor of my best friend Kathy's house and watched her husband, Scott, a quadriplegic, working with his service dog, T-Rex. T-Rex did everything Scott needed him to do, without Scott's having to ask. And Scott knew when it was time to give his dog a scratch behind the ear or when he needed to take a short break. When work was over, T-Rex fetched the television remote and Scott settled in to watch his show. T-Rex lay down in front of Scott's wheelchair and rested his head on Scott's feet. The dog rolled his eyes upward for a quick visual check just as Scott looked down, and between them passed a look that clearly conveyed adoration, love, healing, and, most of all, trust.

Of all the reasons Choice Teaching works so well, I believe that the trust it instills is the most important. T-Rex isn't always perfect and neither is Scott. What they are is perfect for each other, trusting without hesitation.

Don't let anyone other than you and your dog decide what's important in your relationship. My friend Brian has a handsome dog who loves to walk at the end of his leash, maybe even pulling ahead a smidge. People stop Brian all the time to tell him how he can correct that behavior so that his dog heels nicely. The problem is, Brian likes it when his dog forges ahead. He loves to feel the dog's power, and he enjoys the way his dog looks as he prances at the end of the leash. As long as your dog doesn't do anything to hurt or inconvenience others, then do what works for the two of you. What matters most is that you and your dog have a relationship that makes you both happy. If you do, you are experiencing one of life's great gifts.

CHAPTER THIRTEEN

Partners

Nick died on a Thursday. He had lived for twelve years, and in those years he made an indelible mark on me and all those whose lives he touched. Of course, I was distraught. This was a pain so deep that it was difficult to share even with the people I love. It was mine alone, and day after day it battered me. It is said that time heals all wounds. A year after Nick's death in the fall of 2004, I was still waiting for that time to arrive.

In a kind display of condolence, my sister gave me a puppy several months after I lost Nick. I named him Jack and fell in love with him almost immediately. Still, he wasn't Nick. One day Jack and I were headed for a presentation to a philanthropic club, a group of women who informally called themselves the "ladies who lunch." They had a substantial amount of money to donate and were considering several possible charities as the recipient of their largesse. The decision was to be made immediately following my talk. As always, Canine Assistants needed the money very badly. I was under such pressure to make these women understand what a difference our dogs could make in the lives of so many in need that I felt like I was suffocating. So much was riding on that twenty-minute speech. I wanted my Nick. What I had was Jack, an eleven-month-old gold-endoodle.

The parking lot of the bank where the meeting was to be held was full of expensive cars and SUVs. I pulled into a spot, closed my eyes, and thought, *Nick, please help me somehow to get this big goofy puppy through this presentation.* Since Nick's passing, I was constantly talking to him in my mind. Fortunately, I wasn't nutty enough to expect him to answer. Today I was worried about Jack performing well in front of this important audience. Jack knew his "tricks," but offering a paw and flipping a switch would not be enough this afternoon. I needed a dog who could charm the Chanel suits and Manolo Blahniks right off these women. I needed Nick. He would have wowed them. He always did. Nick put something special into my presentations, and the crowd always loved it. He would cover his eyes if my voice got weepy, bark loudly when I asked him if he loved me, and, if he felt I was going on a bit too long, he would pick up my purse and make his way to the exit door. People would roar with laughter and open their hearts and wallets to Canine Assistants.

My speech was going well enough. Jack had been particularly charming as we entered the room, offering his paw to each lady in turn. As I told the story of my father, I started to tear up. I was astonished and dismayed when most of the women giggled at my tears. I couldn't understand their reaction—until I looked down at Jack and saw the cause of their laughter. Jack had covered his eyes with his paws, just as Nick used to do. Since Jack had never batted an eye at my tears before, I dismissed his antics as coincidence and continued with my talk. Toward the end of my remarks, I again heard the ladies laughing. Jack had quietly picked up my purse and was making his way to the door. Jack had never before put my purse in his mouth.

I cannot explain what happened that morning. My head says it was a coincidence, but my heart says otherwise. I no longer try to make sense of it. I just accept the incredible sense of peace it gives me.

• • •

What is it that makes dog and man love each other so much that even death cannot break their bond? Part of it is purely chemical. Oxytocin, the "love" hormone, is released into the bloodstream when humans stroke dogs. Dogs, too, seem to get a heightened level of oxytocin when we touch them.

Dogs and humans are both highly social, highly emotional species. We are designed to seek out partners. It seems only natural then that we would bond to one another. As Patricia McConnell notes in *For the Love of a Dog,* the primary emotion that dogs express is happiness, and happiness is contagious. Who wouldn't want to be around someone who makes you happy?

Finally, we love dogs because we trust them to love us, to forgive us, to comfort us, to take our side even when we are woefully in the wrong. Our dogs don't give us "constructive criticism." They don't say things like "there are two sides to every story" when we recount the error of another's ways. They think more of us than we think of ourselves. They love us more than we love ourselves.

Dogs benefit from the relationship too. Most dogs will seek out human company even before that of other dogs. They know that man can provide and care for them in ways other dogs cannot, and they maintain the unwavering hope that we will do so—if not today, maybe tomorrow.

That doesn't mean that relationships between people and dogs are always easy. There were times when Nick and I got awfully upset with each other. One day we were completing the filming of a segment for a national television program. The filming of this two-minute piece had taken three days, and the schedule was grueling. The producers wanted Nick to look as if he were playing the guitar and painting a picture, with the paintbrush held between his toes. He was a golden retriever, so his toes were webbed, for heaven's sake. He couldn't hold a guitar pick or a paintbrush. As they pressured me, I, in turn, pressured Nick. They finally settled for him holding the guitar pick, and later the paintbrush, in his mouth. When at last they called it a wrap, Nick leapt into the cargo area of the car, though he usually sat in the seat just behind mine, and plastered his nose to the back windshield as if he couldn't stand the sight of me. However, as is typical of dogs, all was forgiven by the time we got home.

Nick's I-will-get-you-before-you-can-get-me attitude with other dogs often caused me anxiety. Although it got better over time, Nick always preferred the companionship of people to that of dogs—unless those people came into our home or yard without permission, in which case Nick treated them like unwelcome dogs. Some days I had my hands full keeping him out of trouble. I am certain he felt much the same way about me. Though we both had our flaws, those imperfections seemed to increase our attachment rather than diminish our love. We both agreed that perfection was obnoxious; neither of us had to worry.

While our relationship may not always have been easy, it was always worth it. It became far easier as we came to understand each other. Nick learned what made me relax, and he would remain close but quiet when it was best to stay out of my way for a few minutes. My husband used to get an alert from Nick if I was upset when I came home. Often without even seeing my face, Nick could tell if I was unhappy or distressed about something the moment I walked through the door. At those times he would softly withdraw to the bedroom until I had a chance to unwind. And I learned what scared Nick and what made him happy. Along the way, I learned some truths about dogs. That knowledge has led me to another truth, this one about me: I am not a dog trainer. I consider myself more of a counselor—a relationship expert, if you will.

What follows are some of the fundamentals of the dog–human relationship that I have learned over time. I call them dogisms.

Dogs do not deliberately do things to anger or frustrate you. The rapid and successful evolution of dogs indicates that the species has excellent survival instincts. They have spent thousands of years carefully studying humans in an effort to make us happy so that we will continue to care for them. They don't tear up your sofa cushions as a punishment because you left them alone. They tear up the sofa cushions because they are anxious or they need to chew or they are bored.

Many people refuse to believe this. They insist that their dogs seem to act guilty when they have misbehaved. Not true. All your dog really knows is that the last time you, he, and poop were gathered together in the same house at the same time, things did not go well for him. He has no clue what specifically he did that was wrong. Understanding that an action will cause consequences at some point in the future suggests an advanced level of cognition that is simply not part of a dog's mental processes.

Dogs do not speak human. Can you imagine bringing a foreign exchange student, who does not speak your language, into your home and popping them on the nose with a newspaper when they don't understand your instructions? You'd be arrested. But that's what we do with our dogs. While research has shown that dogs can learn to recognize approximately 160 words, we commonly forget when we peer into their wise-looking eyes that these beautiful creatures do not share our spoken language. Saying "Don't pee on the rug" or "Don't chew up my glasses" to your dog is basically wasted oxygen and effort. In order to have any valid expectations of dogs' behavior, we must be sure that either dogs understand us clearly or we have made the possibility of committing an infraction physically impossible. If you don't want your dog to eat your glasses, don't leave your glasses where your dog can get them. If you are worried about bathroom accidents, keep your dog in a crate when you are gone. It is all incredibly simple if we just take responsibility for being the "smarter" species and stop expecting our dogs to behave in ways that are beyond their abilities.

Dogs associate behaviors with situational specificity. What I mean by situational specificity is that dogs take into consideration the contextual components of any situation, such as who is speaking, the environment, and the location. A dog who knows that he should put his bottom on the floor when Mary says "Sit," in her high-pitched voice, may be totally clueless when hearing the same word in Bill's deep baritone voice. Situational specificity also means that a dog who understands "sit" when told to sit on grass may not understand that the same movement is required when asked to sit on concrete. Weird as it may seem, it makes a great deal of sense when you remember that *dogs don't speak our language.* However, it is possible to teach a dog to generalize—to understand that a request for a behavior means the same thing no matter who says it or under what circumstances it is said. But don't assume your dog knows the command until he has proven it in many different settings. Ever wonder why a dog has trouble learning that "sit" from a standing position means the same thing as "sit" from a down position? It's because the two involve totally different movements. Dogs assume that the *motion of a behavior* is what is being cued, not the resulting position.

I trained Casey, a very nice black Lab, for a young woman named Molly, who has cerebral palsy. Speaking (barking) was to be an important part of Casey's behavioral repertoire; he would bark when Molly needed to summon her mother or father. Wouldn't you know it? Casey wouldn't speak. No matter what I tried, I simply could not get the dog to vocalize. One day Casey was in a nearby crate as I worked another dog. He watched intently as I gave the other dog a play break complete with toys and treats. Sure enough, Casey could not stand being excluded from all the action, and he let out a beautiful bark. I was so excited and praised Casey profusely for his "speak," rewarding him with multiple treats. He seemed to understand my praise—or at least the treats. He repeated the bark five or six times before I felt confident enough to show his new skill off to the rest of the staff. I ran into our main office, shouting, "Casey can speak! Come see!" I went over to Casey's crate and let him out to visit with everyone. Then I said to him, "Speak." Casey ran into his crate, turned around so he was facing outward, and barked. That's situational specificity.

.

Rarely does a dog know better than to do what he is doing. When you think, *He knows better than that,* I'd ask you to stop and evaluate the situation as your dog likely perceives it. I recently spoke to a woman whose dog was recovering from having been hit by a car. She told me she was shocked when the dog later ran into the street toward a neighboring child who was calling to him. "He knows better than to do that," she said. Really? How exactly did she train him not to leave the yard when he's being called? Consider how incredibly difficult it would be to teach a dog to never, under any circumstances, leave the yard. Despite the ability of dogs to generalize behavior requests, it is virtually impossible to teach them "do not leave the yard no matter what." There are just too many aspects to generalize. You would have to teach the dog never to step over an imaginary boundary that encircles the entire yard. Or you could put him on a long "down–stay," but what happens if another person gives the dog a different command? Or a cat races past? Dogs will be dogs, first, foremost, and forever. There are simply too many variables and the risks too high to feel comfortable that "he knows better."

It is much easier to teach a dog what is acceptable behavior than to teach him what is inappropriate. There are about fifty gazillion (as my son would say) things you would not want your dog to do and a mere handful that you would want him to do. It makes sense then that it is easier to show him what to do rather than the other way around. How many times a day is your dog's behavior perfectly acceptable? How often do you say, "Yes! Way to chew on your toy, Rover!"? People— me very much included—tend to wait until we catch those around us doing something wrong before we provide feedback. When your dog is behaving appropriately, tell him. Your dog is far more likely to repeat a behavior you have shown him makes you happy, because he knows that works for him.

The idea of "because I said so" doesn't work any better for dogs than it does for children. Do not believe that a dog will do whatever you ask without reward unless you have given him good reason to believe that to do so is in his best interest. Dogs, like people, prefer to get something in exchange for their efforts. Don't expect too much for too little. Even mothers would not continue to care for their children if they were not rewarded by occasional bouts of maternal bliss. All creatures need and deserve motivation and reward.

Dogs are dependent upon us for their very survival. When Chase, my son, was about four years old, we passed a dog running along the side of the road. As I tried to find a place to pull my car over so we could pick up the dog, Chase asked me if I thought the dog had an owner.

"I'm not sure, sweetie, but we will find him one if he doesn't," I responded.

"Thank goodness," Chase said. "All dogs need to have a person. They are too poor to be on their own."

It turned out the dog did have an owner, a very frantic one who was out looking for him. The dog had dug a hole under his fence and scooted out for a romp. Not all dogs are that lucky. Dogs need us and trust us to provide for them and keep them safe.

George Eliot wrote, "We long for an affection altogether ignorant of our faults. Heaven has accorded this to us in the uncritical canine attachment." Amen. The opportunity to share our lives with dogs is a gift both of creation and chemistry. It is one we should treasure.

Sadly, we don't always. One day, Mom and I went to the Cobb County animal shelter outside Atlanta, looking to adopt dogs for Canine Assistants. As we waited to go into the kenneling area, a nicely dressed woman came in dragging a beautiful Brittany spaniel. The Brittany was clearly terrified as she first resisted entering the building and then began to try to climb into her owner's arms. The woman screamed, "Take this damn dog. She has messed on my carpet for the last time." As the animal-control officer reached out for the Brittany, the dog growled and tried to bite him.

It was one of the very few times in my life I ever saw my mother explode with anger. "They are going to put your dog to sleep, you know," she shouted at the woman. "She is so frightened that she will keep trying to bite, and they will have no choice but to euthanize her. Is carpet really worth the dog's life?"

A sympathetic officer gently escorted my sobbing mother to our car. I stayed behind, begging the woman to give me the dog, but she insisted on turning her in to the shelter in order to avoid having any liability for her behavior. The shelter could not put the dog up for adoption, because she was so "aggressive," and the beautiful Brittany was destroyed that same afternoon.

Mom and I sat in the parking lot for almost an hour as she cried out her anger and angst. "Why don't people understand that we are responsible for the well-being of living creatures who don't have the ability to care for themselves?" she said. "That precious dog didn't ask to be born. She didn't ask to be sold like a quart of milk to the first person willing to pay the price. How can someone care more for carpeting than for a living, breathing, feeling creature who so obviously loves her? What is that woman teaching her children?" It all poured out. " 'Whatsoever you do unto the least of these, you do also unto me' isn't just a Bible verse," Mom continued. "It is a natural law. Behavior like that woman's makes me afraid for us all. It is a very short step between abusing a dog and abusing a child, between thinking it is acceptable to mistreat an animal and thinking it is acceptable to mistreat other people."

The sentiment hung like a dark cloud over us as we drove home. That Brittany haunts me, not just because she was a lovely creature who did not deserve her fate but because of what she represents— our unwillingness to provide for those we've made dependent upon us. We cannot turn our backs on the covenant we entered into long ago. Thousands of years ago we made a deal that if dogs would work with us, we would provide for them. Dogs have upheld their end of the covenant. Though over time the nature of their work on our behalf has evolved from largely physical to largely emotional, it is no less valuable to mankind. Dogs are of vital importance to people. They are our chosen partners in life. If we do not uphold our end of the agreement, we are violating a natural law, and the consequences for us as a species could be momentous.

Of course, it isn't too late. Our dogs still believe in us. Starting shortly after his first Christmas, Jack brought his toys into my bed as I slept. He would carefully bury them somewhere under me. At first I thought he was delivering gifts and nicknamed him "Santa Paws." Several weeks later I realized that he was indeed giving me gifts, just not the ones I'd thought. He was giving me his valuables to keep safe from the other dogs; he was giving me his trust. Jack, like Nick before him, has confidence that I will protect those things he holds dear—his stuffed squirrel, his knotty rope, and an occasional rawhide. Far more important, he has entrusted himself to me, heart and soul, a gift beyond price.

To borrow a sentiment from singer Helen Reddy, we "know too much to go back and pretend." We know that our dogs are thinking, sentient beings. We know they are not little humans in furry costumes. We know that our dogs do not require physical and emotional domination but they do require our benevolent leadership. We know that dogs are exceedingly bright in certain ways but that they cannot come close to keeping up with our cognitive abilities, so the burden of higher thinking falls to us. We know that our dogs are thoroughly emotional creatures who feel deeply and react quickly to emotional stimuli. We know that it is not acceptable to treat our dogs with anything less than respect and that respect necessitates an understanding of a dog's strengths and limitations. Dogs' brains, sensory abilities, emotions, language, personalities, and character traits belong to a subspecies uniquely their own. They are bright, loving, splendid creatures who deserve to be adored for exactly who and what they are: dogs. We know that we, as people, are responsible for the well-being of dogs—all dogs, not just our own.

Ignorance can no longer be an acceptable excuse for cruelty. This is in no way about "caring more for dogs than for people" or some such nonsense. It is about our morality as a species. Unkindness affects each of us and it diminishes each of us.

I have been told many times in my life, "You can't save them all." Maybe I can't. Maybe. But all of us together can take responsibility for dogs. We can treat them with respect and kindness. We can honor their trust. And we should. It's important—for all of us.

While I was writing this book, my lovely little golden retriever Margaret Ann died. She was named in memory of my mother. Margaret was as sweet and gentle a creature as has ever been born. I long to see her running toward me, ears flopping back in the wind, just one more time. I want to hold her and brush her and feed her. I find that my body aches with my inability to do so. I refuse, though, to believe I have lost her altogether.

Amid all the supportive notes and letters that came when my mother died was one small card that read simply: "For no one loved is ever lost, and she was loved so much." When I read that, I thought, *Yes, of course. That's it.* We loved each other far too much to let death separate us completely. This is how I feel about my precious dogs, most especially my darling Nick. We share a love too strong to ever be destroyed. They are with me always.

Choice Teaching Specifics

Teaching Tips

It may take the dog a few moments to figure out what is wanted, even when you use a lure. Give the cue once and wait for a count of five before repeating. Repeating a cue does not create a dog who responds only after you have given the cue multiple times, unless you use the cues so closely together—such as "sit sit sit"—that the dog interprets them as all part of the same request. The dog will get faster at complying as he better understands the cues.

Additionally, moving the lure around a bit to find the spot most likely to prompt the dog into the desired behavior can also trigger the desired response. It's important to remember that dogs understand body language far better than they understand spoken words.

Dogs must be allowed ample time to decode the words when physical cues are no longer being used and reliance is on only verbal cues. If the dog does not respond to the spoken cue only, it may be necessary to back up and wean more slowly off the physical cue.

Above all else, dogs follow eye movement, so this tool is important to help him understand the cues. Look where you want your dog to look when you cue a behavior. For example, when cueing a "down," look at the dog, then look at the floor while saying the word "down."

Dogs do what is in their best interest—as we all do. Use only positive motivation to convince the dog that it is in his best interest to do as asked. This may mean grilling a steak and using tiny pieces of it or throwing your dog's favorite toy as a reward.

Vary your rewards to keep things exciting. Use the dog's daily food ration for behaviors that are easier to train, and break Milk-Bone's soft treats into small pieces for more-difficult ones. Never use the same treat more than five times in a row. Cheese, peanut butter, toys, balls, belly rubs, or even cat food—whatever the dog likes—can serve as supplements for standard rewards. Edible treats have calories, so if they are used, adjust the dog's food and exercise accordingly.

Go to a random reward schedule *as soon as* the dog knows a behavior well.

In some circumstances, the dog may feel too vulnerable to perform certain behaviors, especially when around other dogs. Try moving him somewhere he feels safer or, at least, allowing him extra time to get comfortable enough to comply.

Always check your own body position relative to the dog's position when asking for a behavior that requires movement; you should not be in his way.

The dog may feel that trying to perform is hopeless if he has been unable to please you in the past. When dogs give up, they often look away as if totally uninterested. If this happens, ask the dog to do something at which he excels, then praise him like crazy. Making the dog feel successful is a key component in the educational process.

You must get a dog "on the phone" (paying attention to you) before cueing a behavior. There are many ways to get a dog's attention, such as by calling his name, rattling a treat bag, or waving a toy. Let the dog "hang up the phone" every few minutes. It is exhausting, mentally and physically, for a dog to have to concentrate on every little nuance as you teach him. Let him relax by giving him thirty seconds or so of scratching or rubbing. At Canine Assistants, our dogs all seem to go for the water bowl, thirsty or not, when they need a break. They quickly learn that no one minds if you need a drink of water. Anticipating their need for breaks prevents them from having to create their own distraction.

Teaching can and should be a daily, ongoing process throughout your relationship with your dog. Specific sessions should never exceed about twenty minutes in length for adult dogs and ten minutes for puppies. If you and the dog both want to keep working after this time as passed, take a five-minute break and start a new session.

Vary distraction levels as the dog's skill at each behavior increases. For example, when teaching a dog to "stay," start in a small, quiet room and over time progress to a noisy, crowded park.

Always quit while you're ahead. We stop after the first time our dogs have done a new behavior and after two or three repetitions of a previously known behavior.

Timing is all-important. Dogs can respond to stimuli in less than twelve milliseconds, so be sure you tell the dog he did the right thing with a happy "Yes!" or other marker the second the dog completes the behavior. But don't mark the behavior too soon, or you will end up teaching the dog to crouch when you want him to lie down. (I did this when I was first working with Nick.)

When dogs learn a new behavior, it is the movement that they learn, not the end result. That is why it is often tricky to get a dog to "sit" from a "down" position. Be patient.

Don't let yourself get into the habit of always asking for one behavior after another, unless they belong together. For example, if you always ask your dog to "sit" and then "down," he will start to anticipate the "down" and do it every time you ask for a "sit."

Remember that things often jell for a dog overnight, so if you stop on a positive note, you may find that the dog is even better the following morning.

The following are the cues and behaviors every dog should know.

MARKERS (Words you use to tell your dog that he is on the right track)	WHEN TO USE
"That's it!"	Use this marker as your dog is in the process of doing as you asked.
"Yes!"	Use this marker just as your dog finishes performing the behavior you have requested.
"Good dog!"	Use this marker after "yes" or whenever your dog is performing a behavior that doesn't have a quick, clear end point, like "let's go" or "stay."
"Ainck."	Use this "wounded duck" noise to let your dog know that he is about to do the wrong thing. Always follow this by cueing a behavior he can do, so you end on a positive note!

SPOKEN CUE (Behavior)	PHYSICAL CUE	TEACHING TIPS
Dog's name (Pay attention to you)	Kissing noise or clapping hands gently	The cues will teach this behavior easily. Your dog does NOT have to make eye contact with you. Subtle signs of attention, like an ear cocked toward you, are fine.
Come here (Dog runs to you)	Noise like clapping or whistling or rattling a treat bag as you turn away from your dog	Start with the dog a very short distance from you. Also, turn in the direction you want your dog to go.
Better hurry (Go to the bathroom)	Point to appropriate toileting area.	You must take the dog out at times it is likely he will need to toilet and teach him cues when he is about to perform the behavior on his own.
Wait (Your dog should pause until you ask him to move)	Arm closest to dog should be extended and lowered as close to dog's chest as possible.	Your dog should pause at every threshold, including those at doors, gates, and door of crate.
Kennel (Go into your crate, please)	Point with cue hand into crate.	Gently toss your lure into crate. Then wait for your dog to go into kennel before rewarding.

SPOKEN CUE (Behavior)	PHYSICAL CUE	TEACHING TIPS
Let's go (Move along beside you on a loose leash)	A step forward with the leg closest to your dog	Give your dog treats as you are walking rather than when you finish walking. If your dog puts any tension on the leash at all, stop. Stand still until he comes back toward you and either sits or looks you in the face. (See Appendix B, under "A Tiger by the Tail," for tips if you are having trouble with this behavior.)
Leave it (Ignore whatever you are keying on—like food on the floor, another dog, a child with a cookie, etc.)	A hand across dog's nose, moving away from the object of the "leave it"	Start by holding a treat in your non-lure hand and asking your dog to "leave it," while you use a treat in your lure hand to draw the dog's attention in the opposite direction. Then move on to an item on the floor, other animals, etc.
Off (Please place all four paws on the floor)	Look away from your dog and go limp to get your dog to move "off" of you. For "off" from an object (like a table), move lure hand from dog's nose toward floor.	Remember, "down" means lie down, please, and "off" means four paws on the floor.

SPOKEN CUE (Behavior)	PHYSICAL CUE	TEACHING TIPS
Trade (I'll give you what I am holding if you give me what you are holding)	Show your dog a treat while you reach out to touch what he has in his mouth. When he starts to open his mouth, remove the object and give him the treat.	If your dog is at all food possessive, do not try to teach this behavior without professional help.
Watch me (Look up at my face, please)	Hold a treat between your eyes to teach this behavior. Once your dog automatically looks at your face when you ask him to "watch me," eliminate the lure and just give the reward.	"Watch me" is a command that will help you in many different situations, like when your dog sees a squirrel and considers bolting. Practice this until it is so ingrained in your dog's mind that he will do it regardless of distractions.
Okay (You may now get up from your "stay")	Throw hands out and up and fingers extra spread and palms facing dog.	Some dogs will need the encouragement of a pat of your leg or the rattle of a treat bag to believe that it is truly okay to move. For most, however, this command pretty much teaches itself.

SPOKEN CUE (Behavior)	PHYSICAL CUE	TEACHING TIPS
Back (Take one or more steps backward)	Cup lure hand with back facing dog and make slight shoo motion with fingers.	Practice this behavior with your dog in all sorts of positions relative to you— like beside you and in front of you. Start, however, with your dog facing you so that you can step into him to encourage "back" if he isn't getting it with the physical cue alone.
Fix (Untangle your leash, please)	Place lure hand in front of dog's chest, cupped with palm up, and move slightly up and down.	To teach this, start by wrapping the leash around the lower part of the dog's leg. Grab both ends of the leash in your non-lure hand and jiggle, while giving the physical cue with your lure hand, until the dog's paw falls off the leash.
Go to bed (move onto bed and "down")	A finger of the lure hand pointing toward bed	Walk your dog into this command initially by moving with him to the bed and then giving the "down" cue. Slowly reduce the distance you move with him and eliminate the cue for "down."

SPOKEN CUE (Behavior)	PHYSICAL CUE	TRAINING TIPS
Go in (direct the dog under the table at which you are sitting and into the down position)	A finger of the lure hand pointing under the table	If your dog is at all anxious, you may want to wait a few moments before you ask for this behavior. As with "go to bed," initially ask your dog to "down" once he gets under table and then slowly wean him off the "down" cue. You may toss the lure under the table initially, as you do with "kennel."
Car	Point to opening in vehicle with finger of lure hand	Toss lure into car initially, then pretend to toss lure in and reward only when dog gets in car. If your dog shows any fear about getting into car, pick him up (or have someone pick him up) and put him in car, until he seems to want to get in on his own. Do not repeatedly ask your dog to "car" if he is hesitant or encourage him strongly, as that will only mark "car" in his mind as a big deal.
Dress (dog puts head through collar)	Holding out collar	Lure dog's head through the collar by holding collar between dog's muzzle and the lure in your hand.

Common Behavior Problems

Misbehavior—meaning behavior by the dog that is deemed unacceptable—is influenced by three main factors:

- PERSONALITY: A dog's predisposition to exhibit a behavior.
- EXPERIENCE: A dog's previous experiences.
- ENVIRONMENT: The particular contextual situation at that time.

We can try to prevent misbehaviors by helping our dogs make the best of their personality traits, giving them varied and positive experiences, and trying to keep them out of situations that might invite them to act out. No matter what we do, all dogs misbehave at some point in their lives. How you handle your dog's misbehaviors will determine how likely he is to repeat them.

It's a Dog-Meet-Dog World

If your dog expresses concern when he sees another dog, you must first acknowledge that he is trying to tell you something. Ask him, "Do you see that dog?" Tell him how he should react. "He looks nice!" Be sure to match your voice tone and body language with your words (since, most likely, he does not understand your exact words), keeping a loose leash so your dog does not feel tension or pain. Then reward your dog with a treat or other positive reinforcement for alerting you to a potential danger and responding appropriately.

If your dog continues to behave as if he is upset and the approaching dog is safely restrained, ask your dog to put his front paws on your chest, as that will make your dog taller and more tightly connected to you, two things that will give him more confidence.

If the other dog is not well controlled or is off leash and appears aggressive, ask your dog to "down" and "watch me" or "leave it." If you can put your dog in a submissive posture (down) and have him avoid making eye contact with the other dog, it is unlikely the dog will attack.

This technique also works when your dog barks at other things, like a person with a crazy hat or men with beards. First acknowledge that your dog is telling you something; otherwise he will continue in an effort to get your attention. Then happily explain that you aren't afraid of whatever he sees or hears, keeping your body relaxed and his leash loose. When he is calm, reward him for alerting you and responding appropriately to your directive.

Your primary objective when working with a dog who reacts inappropriately to people or other animals is to move your dog away from fear or anxiety and toward pleasure and happiness. You do this by building positive associations in your dog's mind whenever he sees people or other animals. For example, when Nick saw bearded men, he immediately thought of Milk-Bones. This is an excellent example of classical conditioning—think of Pavlov and his bell.

There Are Monsters at the Door (and Maybe in the Windows and Probably Under the Bed), but I Will Slay Them for You

Dogs want to keep us safe. Security provision has been among dogs' greatest gifts to humans. However, it can be problematic if you don't need protecting. Remember Chapter Three, when Fluffy wouldn't let Grandpa into the house? You can get Grandpa safely into the house if you follow these easy steps:

1. Acknowledge your dog's alert so she won't think you've missed the point. In a light and happy voice say something like, "Who's there? Good girl, Fluffy. It's Grandpa—oh, great news!" (This will make Grandpa feel happy too and may result in a greater inheritance, thus making Fluffy a really good girl!)
2. Don't expect Fluffy to accept Grandpa as her friend and therefore allow him to take liberties such as touching her. This must be determined by Fluffy, not you. All you can do is explain that you want Grandpa in the house.
3. Don't pick up or restrain your dog, which creates a feeling of helplessness, when she's barking, unless you truly believe the situation is out of control.
4. Ask your guests to look at you and not at the dog. If they stare at the dog, they are making a territorial issue a personal one.
5. Develop a positive word that your dog learns to associate with good things, like "friend." Give your dog a great treat when you say "friend." Keep the treats somewhere you can grab them on your way to the door. I like using small treats dipped in peanut butter for this, as it's hard to think about things too much with peanut butter on the roof of your mouth. After you acknowledge your dog's warning, say "friend" and give your dog a treat. Use treats every time you say "friend" for the first eight or ten times and then sporadically after that. If you use treats too many times in a row, your dog will expect a treat whenever anyone comes to your door. Preferable to eating the guests, certainly, but that might prove annoying (and fattening) in the long run.

If your dog usually likes treats but won't take any when guarding, be *very* careful. This is a warning that your dog is most distressed, and you should be prepared to give up training for the short term to protect your dog and your guest. If you have any doubt as to whether or not you can ensure your guest's safety, please consult an APDT (Association of Pet Dog Trainers)–certified trainer in your area. Confirm that the trainer uses only positive reinforcement techniques.

You may find that your normally placid dog exhibits this guarding behavior when circumstances have changed in your home. New babies, new roommates, or even renovations—anything that upsets the status quo—may make your dog more likely to feel the need to guard.

Leaving the Seat Up

Inappropriate elimination, as it is known in polite circles, is one of the most common behavior problems. There are four primary reasons that dogs have accidents in the house:

- They cannot hold it.
- They do not understand exactly where the restroom is.
- They are marking property or territory.
- They are using urine in an effort to elicit caregiving behavior from you.

Dogs need to know exactly where their bathroom is. There are about nine million places you do not want them to go and a scant few you do. Show them where, usher them to the spot, encourage them with a phrase such as "better hurry," and reward them when they go. Give them lots of praise for going in the right spot. Increase your chances of a successful bathroom run by taking them out first thing in the morning and after they eat. Crate training (see Appendix D for tips on crate training) can help tremendously with bathroom issues.

Remember, puppies have tiny bladders. They need to pee frequently. Older dogs often have to go more frequently as well.

Dogs want to keep their dens clean, but what constitutes the den to your dog is limited to the areas where you sleep or hang out. Dogs that run into the seldom-used rooms in the house, like the formal dining room or the living room, to potty are trying to be polite. If you don't go into certain rooms very often, consider blocking them until your dog's bathroom problem is resolved.

Be sure you clean any areas in your house where your dog has gone to the bathroom with something specially designed for the purpose, such as Simple Solution, so that you completely eliminate the smell. Avoid using ammonia products—they will make the area smell even more like a bathroom.

Neutered dogs rarely feel the need to mark indoors. If your dog does, you must catch him in the act. Tell him "No!" in a sharp, firm tone. (Don't yell: It's counterproductive.) Then lead him outside to explain that all marking is to be confined to the outdoors. If you have an unneutered dog, neuter him. Neutered dogs live longer and are healthier.

If you have a dog who pees every time she sees people—called submissive urination—take heart. She will most likely grow out of it. Young dogs, especially females, don't have great muscle control. When they get excited, they simply can't hold their urine. Greet her where you don't have carpet if possible, or plan ahead by putting down a towel. Ignoring the dog or punishing her, as some trainers recommend, is mean, since this is something she cannot yet control.

As I explained in Chapter Three, younger dogs occasionally use urination to show submission to you or to another dog, a behavior most likely designed to indicate "I'm just a baby." This behavior probably comes from their newborn stage, when they could not urinate or defecate until their mothers licked them in the urogenital area. Dogs that urinate for this reason are attempting to acknowledge your leadership, not annoy you. This phase usually ends by about eighteen months of age at the very latest. The most effective means of dealing with this issue is to show her that you'll care for her before she can pee. Send her to get your slippers or her ball as soon as you walk in the door, to both distract her and give her your attention. Using baby talk with these dogs seems to exacerbate the problem and should be avoided.

Feast or Famine

Sneaking food, or "counter surfing," is one of the easiest problems to resolve. There is one simple rule to keep your dog from grabbing food off tables and countertops: *Don't leave food out where the dog can get it.* When you are in the same room, you can instruct your dog to "leave it," and, provided you've worked on your training with him, he should. But nothing that hunts for a living will leave available food untouched unless they are not hungry, and even then they may take what's available. While dogs are no longer wolves, they are still predatory, hunting animals, so when you are out of their sight, all bets are off.

If you insist on leaving food out in available areas, you have two choices:

- Make your dog afraid of the surfaces on which you leave food. (Not suggested.)
- Make your "leave it" become so automatic that your dog will not touch anything without your permission.

Chews vs. Choos

Chewing is natural for dogs. Provide lots of chew toys, but avoid the ones that look similar to items that are inappropriate, such as a slipper. Dogs usually get in trouble for chewing because they are bored. Leave your dog crated if you have to be gone for an extended period of time, so that he doesn't make a chew toy out of your cabinets or furniture. Praise him for chewing on suitable items and, if you catch him chewing on something inappropriate, substitute an appropriate toy. The best way to keep your dog from chewing your shoes or other personal items is to put them out of reach. To a dog, most items are chewable, so don't expect him to be able to tell the difference between his chews and your Jimmy Choos.

Rubber Kong-type toys are an easy way to satisfy your dog's need to chew and to eliminate boredom. I feed my dogs from their Kongs. I mix their kibble up with low-fat cottage cheese and then put the Kong in the freezer for a few hours. I give the dogs their Kongs when I leave for work in the morning and again when I return from work (after I take them out to potty), in order to have an hour of peace and quiet. This is also a good way to keep your dog from inhaling his food.

Here, Boy!

Getting your dog to come when called can be problematic. When a dog is off leash and outdoors, the last thing he usually wants to do is go back on leash or inside. First I am going to describe how to prevent recalls from becoming a problem. Whenever you let your dog off leash, in your yard or at a dog park, you should call him to you every forty-five seconds or so. When he comes, lean down and give him a treat and a pat. Immediately clip on his leash. Then undo his leash and tell him, "Go play!" In this way, your dog will learn that being called gives him the chance to earn a reward but doesn't always mean the good times are over.

Remember, when calling your dog, it is best to angle your body so it appears you are going to walk in the opposite direction from him. When you move toward your dog, he simply assumes—sensibly so—that you and he are both headed in his direction. Never chase your dog when trying to get him to come toward you, or he will imagine you are playing a game. Rather, if you *want* to play chase, run in the opposite direction, so your dog becomes the chaser and not the chased.

Do not be upset if the dog fails to come galloping straight to you when called. Many dogs will take a meandering route when executing recalls. Heading directly toward someone is considered very impolite by dogs. So unless your dog has figured out that you are okay with his taking that kind of social liberty, be prepared to watch him come at you in a circuitous manner. And be happy your dog is polite enough to do so. Avoid using a harsh voice when calling your dog. Nobody wants to head toward someone who sounds angry. Never punish your dog for taking a long time in coming to you. You want his association with returning to your side to be a totally positive one.

If you have trouble getting your dog to come when called, join the club. I used to have a serious problem getting my golden retriever Nan to come inside when our neighbor, Melissa, was outside throwing the ball for her. I would look like a nut, standing outside calling Nan in a singsong voice, shaking the bag of treats, and bolting off in the direction opposite hers. None of it worked. Finally, I realized that I'd set both Nan and myself up to fail. Of course playing ball with her friend was more fun than coming inside with me.

I had two choices. Knowing it is vital that a dog has one behavior that she will do on cue no matter what the circumstances, I had spent many hours teaching Nan to drop in place when I said, "Down." So I could either ask Nan to "down" and walk out and get her, or I could ask Melissa to end the ball game when she saw me. I used both methods at various times, and they both worked well. Sometimes we have to use our big brains to figure out a way to work around the fact that even the best dogs occasionally suffer from a loss of hearing.

A Tiger by the Tail

Pulling on the leash, or forging, is another problem that can be easily corrected if you will be patient enough to retrain your dog. Here are the steps:

1. Allow your dog off leash in an enclosed indoor area. With a handful of small treats, pat your left thigh to encourage your dog to come close to your side.
2. When he does, give him a treat reward and take a step forward. If he steps with you, give him a quick treat and take another step forward.
3. If he runs off, fine. Stand totally still except for an occasional wave of the treat you should have in your hand. Wait for him. He will come back to you—and when he does, repeat step 2.
4. If your dog runs off, it is helpful if you can have someone time how long it takes him to return to your side. You will be shocked to see how quickly the length of his absence shortens.
5. Once your dog is staying close to you, it is time to connect the leash.
6. Take one step forward with your dog and stop. Wait for your dog to make eye contact with you, then take another step forward. Give him a treat as you are stopping.

7. When he consistently makes eye contact or sits within a fast count of two beats, begin taking two paces at a time.

8. Double your steps each time he sits or makes eye contact under the two-beat limit.

9. When you have successfully reached sixteen paces, head outside to a quiet area and repeat the process from step 5.

10. When you have reached sixteen paces in a quiet outdoor environment, head to an area with distractions and, once again, repeat the process from step 5.

11. Once you have successfully completed step 9, you can begin to take short "walks." At random, slow down or stop to keep your dog focused on you.

If your dog pulls on the leash only when he sees other creatures, practice the "watch me" command as you are walking. When your dog watches you, give him a treat. If you have a dog who goes crazy when he sees another dog, you will need to come up with a behavior that will not allow him to pull on his leash and lunge. My favorite is to ask the dog to "front"—that is, make him sit facing you. When he is looking at you and has his back to the oncoming excitement, you will have much better control. Do this every time you spot anything that might make him go nutty. If you practice "front" enough, it will become his automatic response to seeing another creature, thus taking the place of pulling and lunging. Neat trick, but it does take patience and loads of practice.

Huggers and Muggers

The best way to keep your dog from jumping on you and others is to teach him as a young puppy to "sit" when greeting a human. If it's too late for that, then you are going to have to be patient. The best way to eliminate jumping is to ignore your dog when he displays this behavior. Greet him only after he responds appropriately to your "sit" cue. In addition, you can try yelping when he jumps up. Dogs—puppies, in particular—are programmed to receive information about appropriate behavior from their consorts and caregivers. Yelping as if seriously wounded would be extremely distressing to most dogs. You can turn away after you yelp, as if to say, "I am not going to be your friend anymore, because you hurt me!" Obviously, you don't want your dog to think you'll never forgive him, so after turning your back for a few seconds, ask your dog to "sit" and then greet him effusively. Jumping is a behavior that can be corrected, but it takes time, work, and, once again, patience.

Growling and Biting

Dogs have the right to growl. How else can they say "back off" or "ouch"? When your dog growls, it is up to you to determine the cause of his distress. Immediately discontinuing the stimulus is the obvious and safest course. For example, if he growls when you pull his tail, stop pulling his tail. We feed licks of peanut butter when teaching a dog to allow us to handle his paws. The treat makes him begin to positively associate having his paws touched. The stickiness of the peanut butter gives him something else on which to focus.

Nothing is worse than being uncomfortable about your safety around your own dog. If you are the least bit concerned that your dog might bite you, get help immediately. Find an APDT trainer in your area who shares your general philosophy about dogs and hire him or her. The vast majority of trainers who have worked hard enough to become APDT certified are very good at what they do and are perfectly qualified to help you. If you are worried the trainer will say something awful, like "You should put this dog to sleep," remember you are under no obligation to take the advice. The experts should not say this unless there is some extreme mitigating circumstance. If you need additional help, ask your veterinarian for a referral to an animal or veterinary behaviorist.

Important to Note:

- If your dog has bitten you for any reason other than being in severe pain, you need more help than I can give you in a book. Please contact your veterinarian for a referral to an animal or veterinary behaviorist.
- If your dog has ever bitten another person, his life is in your

hands. Keep him away from other people until you can see a behaviorist for a behavior-modification plan.

- Never allow dogs around crawling babies or toddlers. The risk of an "accidental" bite—where the dog instinctively responds to a threat, real or imagined—is too high. That doesn't mean you must give your dog away if you have a baby. That's just silly. Use baby gates to keep children and dogs away from each other, particularly when the child is on the move. Again, it is your job to protect your dog.

Remember, changing or eliminating behavior is a long-term project. Why? Bad behaviors display two characteristics:

1. If what you are using to eliminate the problem (your "pressure" on the behavior) is indeed going to be effective, you will almost always see an extinction burst—an increase in behavior—before you see the behavior decline.
2. Problem behaviors almost always have a series of spontaneous recovery periods (when your dog starts doing it again) for seemingly no reason. The good news is that, properly managed, the behavior won't be as bad as it was the time before and will eventually fade away.

In order to eliminate problem behaviors, you must come up with a way to exert "pressure" on the behavior. Pressure simply means anything that makes the behavior less likely to occur in the future.

Let's say your dog is jumping on you uninvited. Here is a possible scenario:

1. Dog jumps on you, nearly knocking you over (problem behavior).
2. You turn your back to dog and break contact (pressure on behavior).
3. Dog jumps higher and a little more excitedly (extinction burst).
4. Dog gets down (temporary extinction).

Two days later:
1. Dog jumps on you with somewhat less force.
2. You turn your back and break contact.
3. Dog jumps a little higher.
4. Dog gets down.

One week later:
1. Dog jumps on you gently.
2. You turn your back and break contact.
3. Dog reaches up a bit more.
4. Dog gets down.

Two weeks later:
1. Dog starts to jump up.
2. You turn your back and break contact.
3. Dog lifts front legs.
4. Dog gets down.
5. The behavior reaches permanent extinction.

It may take a day to reach permanent extinction or it may take months. The important thing is that each time you see spontaneous recovery, the behavior is lessening, even if slightly. Also, watch for those extinction bursts, as they tell you your pressure is going to be effective.

Three things to note:
1. You must not allow the dog to "get away with" the behavior (not apply pressure) while you are trying to eliminate it, or you will see a worsening of the behavior and will have to start over.
2. Your method of "putting pressure" on the behavior should never involve forcing the dog physically or using the leash. You must let the dog decide it is in his best interest to stop.
3. You must always use the same type of pressure, as inconsistency in handling the behavior can cause it to worsen substantially.

Remember, when you are dealing with a problem behavior, it will not go away overnight. But, if handled properly, it will go away.

Play

As discussed in Chapter Eleven, play is a tremendously important part of a dog's life. The benefits are significant both physically and socially. While most play is wholesome and well-intentioned, it can sometimes deteriorate into something less. As most dog owners know, some dog-on-dog play can turn into aggression and ultimately lead to fights. For the sake of your dog's safety, here are some signs that two dogs are playing well together and signs that things are breaking down:

- Play bows are used as a form of metacommunication, telling something about what will happen next. Saying, "This joke is funny," and then proceeding to tell a funny joke is a form of metacommunication. In dogs, the play bow is the most commonly seen form of metacommunication. It means, "What follows is intended only as play."
- In healthy play, you see frequent, short breaks in activity. Continuous, frenetic activity may be a sign that the play session is ramping out of control.
- The stronger of the two dogs is self-handicapping. When a strong young dog plays with an older dog, it is polite for the younger one not to use all of his power during play. For example, the younger dog may tug a rope against his older playmate, but he won't shake his head or really put his weight into it as he might with a more evenly matched opponent. If one player clearly needs to self-handicap but fails to do so, this constitutes unfair play and should be stopped.
- Vocalizations stay in the middle range in terms of tone and pitch. If one dog's vocalizations begin to get lower and lower or higher and higher in pitch and more frantic in tone, a fight is in the making.

- Each dog respecting the communication efforts of the other is vital to healthy play. If one dog is trying to get away and not being allowed to do so, the situation is unhealthy.
- In healthy play, bites are well inhibited and cause no damage or yelping.
- Open mouths and nice loose tails are good indicators of healthy play.
- Role reversals are also important in fair play. One dog is the biter first and the bitten next. As the old saying goes, "Turnabout is fair play." Roles do not have to be split 50–50, though, as long as both parties are happy with their role.
- Watch for increasing vertical—chest to chest—play. Vertical play tends to turn quickly into fights.

It is also interesting to watch one dog invite another to play. Research has shown that a dog will play bow only in front of a dog who is paying attention to him. If the dog isn't paying attention, the dog who wants to play will match the intensity of his efforts to the degree of inattention of his desired playmate. Dogs are awfully smart about the business of playing.

Studies also show that most dogs would rather play with a person than with another dog. We should make every effort to take advantage of our mutual playfulness. It is a great way to bond with our dogs. How should you play with your dog? That's up to you and your dog, as long as the play is fair and fun for both parties. Despite what trainers commonly say, there is absolutely no evidence that people should always "win" when playing with their dog or risk losing leadership status. Dogs know that play is just that—play, complete with role reversals. I caution you only to keep your dog's arousal level reasonable when playing with him. Lots of rumble-and-tumble play, without clear signals between parties and frequent breaks, can lead your dog to "forget" himself and behave inappropriately. So keep yourself and your dog under control. Playing with your dog is physically and emotionally healthy for both of you.

Grooming

When grooming your dog, start by giving him a quick check-over, noting the condition of his eyes, nose, ears, mouth (teeth), paw pads, toenails, and the area behind his tail (may show his stomach is upset).

If his ears are dirty, take ear cleaner and flush them well. Then you can use cotton balls to gently wipe the area outside the ear canal. Never use Q-tips in the ears, as you can accidentally pack wax farther into the canal.

You can use a warm damp rag to wipe sleep out of your dog's eyes.

Then run your hands all over his body, including the chest, stomach, and leg areas, to feel for bumps or swellings.

Next use a brush to comb through his coat, removing tangles, and check for skin redness. With silky long-haired breeds like goldens, pay special attention to the hair behind the ears (when you clean ears, that hair may really mat) and on the inside of the legs. If you encounter mega-mats, you may want to get a groomer's help. It is really easy (says the voice of experience) to cut your dog while trying to remove a mat close to the skin.

Brush your dog's teeth with special toothpaste, available at any veterinary clinic. I find fingertip brushes the easiest to use. Dental care is a vital part of your dog's overall health.

Trim nails if needed. I like to use a small Dremel sander every week to keep the dog's nails nice and short.

If you are going to bathe your dog, and I recommend you do so about every four to six weeks, now is the time to brush his coat. Always groom before bathing, or mats are difficult to remove.

Finish the grooming session with a nice overall scratch and a treat, so your dog will look forward to this time every day.

Grooming is parenting at its most elemental, and it is truly a great bonding experience for you and your dog.

Daily grooming of your dog:

- Allows you to check for problems like bad ears or swellings.
- Puts you in a comforting parenting role, facilitating bonding and control.
- Calms you and your dog.
- Keeps your dog presentable and keeps problems such as mats under control.

Tips for Keeping Your Dog Happy, Healthy, and Safe

A suitable-size crate is a must in the dog-friendly home. Dogs love having a nest of their own. Crates also help your dog be successful in the house by limiting their ability to wander and be naughty.

All of your dog's interactions with her crate should be positive. Feed her in her crate. Give her treats and toys in her crate. Never use the crate as punishment. Without working your way up to long absences, never put her in her crate and leave for an extended period of time. Start by putting her food in the crate with her. Close the crate door, get your keys, and drive around the block. Be gone no more than five minutes. Let her out to greet you and then put her back into the crate, door closed, for about two minutes. Take her out to potty, since you just fed her. If your dog develops a positive association with her crate, it will make life easier.

Once dogs have developed bad feelings about a crate, it is difficult to ever overcome this discomfort. If your dog already has a negative association with her crate, you can substitute an exercise pen or a small room, using the acclimation technique described above.

Never force your dog into a crate or an enclosure of any kind. You must allow her to decide to enter on her own if you are to ever have a crate-loving dog. When you ask her to "kennel" the first few times, it may take her seconds or even minutes to decide to go in. Be patient; it is well worth the effort.

The only collar that should remain on your dog when he is off leash is the quick-release collar. Dogs can choke on any collar that does not release under pressure. When working with your dog, do not attach your leash to only one side of the quick-release collar or it may release at an inappropriate time.

Do not let your dog off leash anywhere except in a safely fenced area. All dogs can get distracted by something, run off, and potentially get hit by a car.

Never, ever, leave your dog in a hot car. Even if it seems just warm to you, your car can heat like an oven, causing your dog to have heatstroke or worse.

A tired dog is a good dog. Exercise your dog, physically and mentally, every day for good health and behavior.

Do not roll your car windows down far enough for your dog to jump out. Never let your dog ride in the back of a pickup truck.

Watch out for hot pavement, as it can burn your dog's paws. Don't play fetch with your dog on paved surfaces; it can shred their paws.

If you live where it gets quite hot or snows frequently, buy booties to keep your dog's paws safe.

Do not leave your dog unattended around swimming pools. Even good swimmers can find themselves unable to get out of the water without help.

Do not ever let your dog eat or drink anything off the ground.

Do not let your dog drink from the toilet.

Put away all medicines, cleaning supplies, antifreeze, and other potential poisons so your dog cannot get to them.

Put away small objects and toys—anything on which your dog could choke.

Don't let your dog chew on knotted rawhides or tennis balls.

Outdoors, be sure to provide adequate shade and water for your dog.

Never take your dog to concerts or fireworks shows. If fireworks displays are held close enough to your home for you to hear indoors, you may want to stay home with your dog.

Do not keep poisonous plants in your house or yard.

Dogs will chew on electrical cords, so please position cords so that your dog can't get to them.

Obesity is the number-one cause of health problems in American dogs. Use your dog's daily ration of kibble to train or entertain him in order to avoid excess weight gain.

Do not let your dog eat "people food" except for things like cheese, peanut butter, hot dogs, and roast beef when being used in a training context. People food can upset your dog's stomach—some food, such as chocolate and grapes, can even be poisonous to your dog.

Know where your closest veterinary emergency clinic is located.

High-quality food is worth the money, because it is more digestible and leads to better health and less waste.

Dogs do feel pain when they are hurt. Find a veterinarian who understands this and is willing to treat pain appropriately.

Personality Profile Impressions Survey

Name/Species of individual being assessed:

Your Name: Date:

Please circle the number that best fits your impression of the individual being assessed.

	1 = LOW					7 = HIGH	
1. Is sociable:	1	2	3	4	5	6	7
2. Is comfortable in a variety of settings:	1	2	3	4	5	6	7
3. Desires control:	1	2	3	4	5	6	7
4. Is warm:	1	2	3	4	5	6	7
5. Is bossy:	1	2	3	4	5	6	7
6. Can adapt to change:	1	2	3	4	5	6	7
7. Is assertive:	1	2	3	4	5	6	7
8. Takes charge:	1	2	3	4	5	6	7
9. Is friendly:	1	2	3	4	5	6	7
10. Is people-oriented:	1	2	3	4	5	6	7
11. Is bold:	1	2	3	4	5	6	7
12. Makes others feel comfortable:	1	2	3	4	5	6	7

13. Is willing to take risks:	1	2	3	4	5	6	7
14. Likes physical contact:	1	2	3	4	5	6	7
15. Is a leader:	1	2	3	4	5	6	7
16. Likes to make the rules:	1	2	3	4	5	6	7
17. Is adaptable:	1	2	3	4	5	6	7

Personality Assessment Scoring Sheet
Plot Totals on Grid

ASSERTIVENESS

Numerical Score on Question 3:   _____

Numerical Score on Question 5:   _____

Numerical Score on Question 7:   _____

Numerical Score on Question 8:   _____

Numerical Score on Question 11:   _____

Numerical Score on Question 13:   _____

Numerical Score on Question 15:   _____

Numerical Score on Question 16:   _____

Total Assertiveness Points: _____

SOCIABILITY

Numerical Score on Question 1:   _____

Numerical Score on Question 4:   _____

Numerical Score on Question 9:   _____

Numerical Score on Question 10:   _____

Numerical Score on Question 14:   _____

Total Sociability Points: _____

VERSATILITY

Numerical Score on Question 2:   _____

Numerical Score on Question 6: _____

Numerical Score on Question 12: _____

Numerical Score on Question 17: _____

Total Versatility Points: _____

Personality Grid

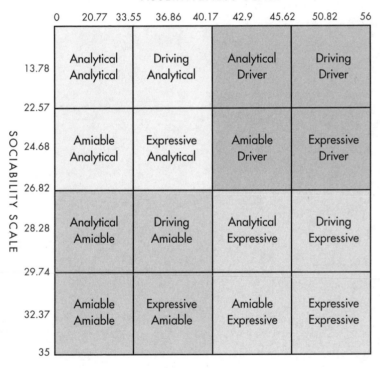

ASSERTIVENESS SCALE

	0 20.77 33.55	36.86 40.17	42.9 45.62	50.82 56
13.78	Analytical Analytical	Driving Analytical	Analytical Driver	Driving Driver
24.68	Amiable Analytical	Expressive Analytical	Amiable Driver	Expressive Driver
28.28	Analytical Amiable	Driving Amiable	Analytical Expressive	Driving Expressive
32.37	Amiable Amiable	Expressive Amiable	Amiable Expressive	Expressive Expressive

SOCIABILITY SCALE: 22.57, 26.82, 29.74, 35

VERSATILITY SCALE

| 0 | 17.59 | 20.08 | 22.43 | 28 |

This book would never have been written, much less published, without the help and support of my brother, Gary. I am both the luckiest sister alive and eternally in his debt. My good luck also extends to the two best sisters a woman could ever have, Katherine and Lisa, both of whom had to hear more about book writing and canine behavior than anyone should and handled it, and me, with their customary love and graciousness. I also owe a debt of gratitude to Dudley, Crawford, T David, Margaret, and Stephen and all the Bruner clan for all their encouragement and support. I thank Mom, Dad, and Nanny for the love they surrounded me with every day. You remain very much alive in my heart.

To Kathy, I owe my sanity, tentative though it may be at times. No woman ever had a better friend or one so loved as you, my BFF. I am a woman blessed with many amazing friends, among them David and Debbie, Gerilyn, and Carolyn, for whom I am both daily and eternally grateful.

A huge thank-you to the staff, board, volunteers, recipients, and animals of Canine Assistants, all of whom I adore. I am particularly indebted to Crawford and Tib for their wise counsel. And to my wonderful Meghan, you are far more than just my right hand, and I hope you know how very much I love and appreciate you—and not just for producing the cutest godson a woman ever had.

To those whose generosity makes Canine Assistants possible, especially everyone at Del Monte/Milk-Bone, UCB, Delta Airlines, and the Looneys, I give my gratitude. You are extraordinary people. Not a night goes by when I don't thank God for you all.

To everyone at PBS, tpt, and Partisan Pictures, I give my complete adoration. Working with you is a privilege, one for which I am supremely grateful. Among the many wonderful things you have done and continue to do, you made it possible for me to meet Michael, a kindred soul, whose light in my life remains undimmed by mere death.

Susan Golomb of the Golomb Agency loved dogs enough to take a chance on me. You are a wonderful friend, teacher, and guide, Susan, and I remain in awe of my good fortune in having you take me under your wing.

To my Julie Grau at Spiegel & Grau, I owe more than words can express. You captured my heart that first day and have held it ever since. I knew from the very beginning you were the one. I thank you for allowing me to work with the extraordinary people at Random House.

To Jack, Butch, and Nan, who remind me every day how truly wonderful dogs are, I give all my love. My love also to Puppy Case, Margaret Ann, Nick, Samantha, and all the other dogs who've crossed the rainbow bridge before me. Remember, it is never good-bye—just see you later, my precious angels.

Finally, I thank my husband Kent and my son, Chase, for all their help and patience during the "Summer of Book" and beyond. I love you both to the moon and back a trillion times over.

Jennifer

ABOUT THE AUTHOR

Jennifer Arnold is the founder and executive director of Canine Assistants, a service-dog school based in Milton, Georgia. She lives with her husband, veterinarian Kent Bruner, son Chase, three dogs, Bob the cat, eight horses, and a number of other animals.

ABOUT CANINE ASSISTANTS

Canine Assistants is a nonprofit organization dedicated to providing service dogs for children and adults who have physical disabilities, epilepsy, or other special needs. Canine Assistants does not charge for the service it provides; rather, it relies on the generosity of those who recognize that helping one benefits us all.

To learn more about this very special program, please visit their website at www.canineassistants.com.

ABOUT THE TYPE

This book was set in Bembo, a typeface based on an old-style
Roman face that was used for Cardinal Bembo's tract *De Aetna* in
1495. Bembo was cut by Francisco Griffo in the early sixteenth century. The Lanston Monotype Company of Philadelphia brought
the well-proportioned letterforms of Bembo to the United States in
the 1930s.